Clem Sunter

Never mind the Millennium. What about the next 24 hours?

Human & Rousseau
Tafelberg

PREVIOUS BOOKS BY THE AUTHOR:
The World and South Africa in the 1990s
South African Environments into the 21st Century
  (with Brian Huntley and Roy Siegfried)
The New Century
Pretoria will Provide and other Myths
The Casino Model
The High Road: Where are we now?
What it really takes to be World Class
Home Truths

First published in 1999 jointly by
Human & Rousseau (Pty) Ltd,
Design Centre, 179 Loop Street, Cape Town,
and Tafelberg Publishers Ltd,
28 Wale Street, Cape Town

© 1999 Human & Rousseau (Pty) Ltd and
Tafelberg Publishers Ltd
All rights strictly reserved. No part of this book
may be reproduced or transmitted in any form
or by any means, electronic or mechanical,
or by photocopying, recording or microfilming,
or stored in any retrieval system,
without the written permission of the publishers

Cover design and typography by Jürgèn Fomm
Typeset in 11.5 on 14pt Palatino. Printed and bound
by National Book Printers, Drukkery Street,
Goodwood, Western Cape, South Africa

First edition, first impression 1999
ISBN 0 7981 3763 0

IN MEMORY OF GAVIN RELLY
A FOX WITH A HEART OF GOLD

Whoso beset him round
With dismal stories,
Do but themselves confound;
His strength the more is.
No lion can him fright;
He'll with a giant fight,
But he will have the right
To be a pilgrim.

JOHN BUNYAN (1628-1688)

A vision turned sour

When I was a teenager in England, the Beatles and the Rolling Stones reigned supreme. London was swinging; ties were broad and printed in a range of psychedelic colours; trousers were bell-bottomed and skirts were mini. I played in a tight little rock band that was very popular on the debutante circuit before the age of discotheques and synthesisers. Jiving had given way to "The Twist" as the latest dance craze and, by and large, it was a fantastic time to be young. On the literary front the steamy novel by D H Lawrence, *Lady Chatterley's Lover*, was unbanned. In real life, Christine Keeler was painted as *la femme fatale* by the English press. On the other side of the Atlantic, Elvis was never the same after he came back from his stint as a GI in Germany. America had moved on to The Beach Boys and surfing. Or else, if you were reaching for a more unconventional lifestyle, you became a hippie who smoked pot and went to San Francisco with flowers in your hair.

Like many others in the 1960s, I was optimistic about the future. After all, I'd been told by Harold Macmillan, the British Prime Minister, that I'd never had it so good. Okay, the other Harold – Harold Wilson – said that a week in politics was a long time; so who can trust a politician? Into the bargain, we had protests over the Vietnam war and Bob Dylan's rasping voice reminding us that we'd better start swimming or we'd sink like a stone. But, on the whole, we looked forward to a better quality of life for ourselves and for an increasing proportion of the world's population. The gap between the rich and the poor would definitely close.

One of the principal reasons for this faith in the future was the awesome advance in technology we were witnessing at the time. The Apollo space programme which would shortly put a man on the moon was in full swing. Meanwhile, on this planet, we had the heady experience of driving around in green-and-white Mini Coopers with transverse engines. On a broader, more philosophical plane, technology was making it easier for people to make things. Because workers were becoming more productive, we looked forward to four-day working weeks. We would have more time for recreation and fun, while robots slaved away in the factories. The stress factor in our lives would diminish and we would be able to manage our leisure time as seriously as we managed our work. In this regard, I remember a remark once made to me by one of my more laid-back "digs" mates: "Nobody said with his dying breath that he should have worked harder." For those less fortunate than ourselves, technology would liberate them from the drudgery of poverty, and allow them to pursue their higher-order spiritual interests. It was the time of Karma and Zen and communing with nature. We were at the dawning of the Age of Aquarius.

So much for the rosy vision of youth! Unfortunately, what has actually happened is quite the opposite. Indeed, less time is required to manufacture a car or a TV set. Human ingenuity has delivered the anticipated gains in productivity; but, instead of workers having more time off to meditate transcendentally, fewer of them are needed. Improvements in technology combined with intense global competition have meant that big businesses everywhere in the world are merging their operations and downsizing their labour forces. The workforce of the largest company in the world, General Motors, has fallen from a peak of 800 000 employees in the 1960s to 600 000 today. GM as well as the other automobile majors are simplifying themselves. They still produce a dazzling variety of models to lure the customer; but, under the bonnet, standardisation and interchangeability of parts are driving unit costs down and diminishing the number of workers required to assemble the car. Even the chassis these days can be common to a range of models and makes. Fifty per cent of Americans worked on assembly lines in the 1960s. Now only 15 per cent do and they produce far more than the 50 per cent ever did. The decline of big business as an employer is an exact replica of the earlier experience of the agricultural industry. The latter employed the majority of Americans in the 1880s and now employs only three per cent. But those three per cent use combine harvesters, fertilisers and biotechnology to produce a regular abundance of crops and animals. We have butter mountains and wine lakes to contend with!

Importantly, one mustn't confuse economic size with employment potential. It's true that companies are getting bigger in terms of profit and market capitalisation. General Electric's market value recently breached the $300 billion barrier. So did Microsoft's. Furthermore, relentless competition is causing companies to join up with one another to realise even greater economies of scale. Latest in line as pairings are Daimler-Benz/Chrysler and Exxon/Mobil. As they say in this dog-eat-dog world, you either do lunch or be lunch! It's also true that service industries are taking over from manufacturing as the primary source of employment. For example, Wal-Mart Stores employ 825 000 staff in the United States. But the general trend of big business as the dominating factor in the average person's lifetime career is in seminal decline. The average Joe or Joanna may still be buying a car, petrol or a refrigerator from big business, or have a contract to supply goods or a service to big business. But the odds are that he or she is no longer in permanent employment in that sector. The little cogs in the big wheels are less numerous these days. Mergers, acquisitions and general shake-outs are destroying jobs on an unprecedented scale. As a by-product, trade union membership has suffered.

To compound the employment problem, governments everywhere are likewise rationalising their civil services and are no longer prepared to act as employers of last resort. I remember my father telling me that if I achieved some semblance of respectability in my "A" Level marks, I could always join the British Civil Service. Not now! Furthermore, privatisation has added to the growing number of redundant civil servants, as bloated parastatals are subjected to the discipline of the marketplace. The slimming of government is in response to taxpayers simply not being prepared to accept any further increases in taxes over and above the ones already being levied on them. Government expenditure has risen from less than five per cent of GDP at the beginning of this century to the present range of between 30 and 60 per cent of GDP. Citizens are therefore calling for a halt to any further rises. Anyhow, Keynesianism is unfashionable. The prevailing wisdom is that public works programmes do not create sustainable jobs. At best, they act as a short-term palliative and only last as long as the money is available to fund them.

So the two great motors of job creation in the 1960s – big business and the public sector – have shut down or have even gone into reverse in the 1990s. One statistic says it all: 93 per cent of school leavers in South Africa currently cannot find work in the formal sector of the economy. Judie Lannon, a remarkable American who lives in London and specialises in social trends, talks of the extreme fragmentation of society that once seemed so coherent. Collectivism is making way for individualism as we convert from a modernist to a postmodernist society. All the old certainties have evaporated and concepts like salaries, pensions, medical aid and lifetime employment are becoming obsolete (having only been around for a hundred years anyway as a temporary aberration).

Pushing the coach of societal change along is the ageing demography of the rich nations. In effect, their citizens were members of a gigantic pyramid scheme which was viable as long as a sufficient number of new entrants were coming in at the bottom. The latter could cross-subsidise the earlier members. However, with the ratio of old and frail to young and healthy ratcheting up all the time, the scheme is now coming seriously adrift. In line with the thinking of Judie Lannon, therefore, companies are fragmenting along both vertical and horizontal fault lines – vertically as they discard non-core businesses and horizontally as they discard non-core functions. With the peripherals gone, what is left is just the bull's-eye – a much diminished permanent workforce containing core employees with core competencies in core business areas. For example, Coca-Cola boils down to the syrup and the brand. Everything else from the bottling to distribution is outsourced.

Shedding costs and therefore people is the name of the game everywhere. Overheads perceived to add no value are particularly coming under the hammer, as we demassify ourselves. The upshot is that the centre of gravity of economic activity is moving back from big to small. We are increasingly reverting to a straight free-market system where you get paid for the hard skills you possess in being a potter, plumber, dentist, accountant, scenario-planner, etc. and for the work you actually perform. Life is a series of contracts rather than one long continuous state of employment. Literally, we are back to piecework where craftsmen and merchants negotiate their fee. Perhaps guilds will have another day. Look at all the suburban homes that are now doubling as business premises because the occupants no longer go to work – they work from home. Overtime and clocking in and out are rapidly becoming things of the past. You choose your own working hours as long as you get the job done on time and to the standard specified.

In order to cope with a market changing faster by the day, people are increasingly viewing jobs like roles in a play. As the curtain comes down on one job, you move on to the next one (the average American does this seven times in his or her working career). Should you be at a loose end between plays, the dole is getting more difficult to get and usually it has an expiry date. When you stop acting altogether, so does the pay you get. In short, the idea that you can live for 80 years, work for half of them in one institution and be looked after – one way or another – for the other forty can no longer be entertained. The 20th-century Humpty Dumpty that we created and called the welfare state will never be put back together again.

Given these radical changes in the structure of industry and employment, there is bound to be a large number of casualties – especially in societies which are slow to adjust to the new realities. In the last respect, Europe comes to mind. Recently, Will Hutton, who was an economics editor at *The Guardian* newspaper in London, described Britain as a 30-30-40 society in a book entitled *The State We're In*. Thirty per cent of British people are excluded from the economic mainstream (the most extreme example of whom you will find living in cardboard boxes under Waterloo Bridge); 30 per cent are included but in insecure jobs; and 40 per cent are basically in safe and permanent employment. If 60 per cent of British society are no longer in jobs that can be described as satisfactory, imagine what that figure is elsewhere in Europe. Remember, Britain got on its bicycle first and is supposed to be ahead of France, Germany and Spain in the process of transformation. More to the point, if Britain suffers from a 60 per cent exclusion rate, what is the figure in South Africa? Seventy per cent? Eighty per cent?

Thus, unemployment is now the scourge of virtually every single nation. As South Korean student, Cho Eun Young, put it so eloquently: "Finding a job is harder than pulling a star out of the sky." The majority of the world's inhabitants have no sense of ownership of their lives, no sense of control as they are buffeted by the winds of globalisation. The news broadcasts talk dismally of economic catastrophe in the Far East that could lead directly to your retrenchment in a little village thousands of miles away. Everything is interconnected. Someone half joked to me the other day that a recession is when other people lose their jobs, a depression is when you lose yours! Alarmingly, the gap between the rich and the poor is actually widening because more and more are joining the ranks of zero income earners. The coefficient which measures inequality between the top and bottom cohorts of income earners is zooming, because any number divided by zero is infinity. The world's richest 350 people have an aggregate fortune greater than the combined wealth of the poorest 45 per cent of the world's population. That's a statistic to make you blink! Rather than too much money in too few hands, it suggests too little money in too many hands.

Meanwhile, those still lucky enough to have jobs are working even harder than their predecessors in the 1960s in order to protect themselves from being made redundant. All in all, I would say that there is a great deal more misery in the world now than when I was a kid. On the one hand, millions of unemployed people have no purpose in life and therefore no self-esteem. On the other hand, millions of employed people are working longer hours and are totally stressed out trying to balance family commitments against work commitments. And this applies equally to men and women, given the blurring of the gender roles. Husbands and wives pass like ships in the night – exhausted into silence by their daytime occupations.

The dream of the 1960s has turned into the nightmare (and daymare) of the 1990s! In saying this, I am not wishing to come across as a neo-Luddite. Technological progress is inevitable, since it's part of the human condition to seek constant improvement. Luddites, you may recall, were a group of people who in the early 19th century went around wrecking machines in northern England. They thought that the advances in technology which precipitated the Industrial Revolution were evil because they put spinners and weavers out of work. Indeed, machines did make a lot of manual workers redundant at the time, but concurrently they created a whole new range of jobs. Job substitution, not destruction, was the result. Likewise, technologies today are imperilling many traditional occupations, but they have the potential of enabling individuals to pursue an incredible number of completely new activities. It's just that we haven't grasped how the nature of employment has to change in order to take advantage of the latest technological wave.

Technology today is on the side of the small, productive person. Microelectronics, information technology and possible new forms of energy generation all favour the entrepreneur. In the first instance, the personal computer is a boon for small business. It comes packed with as much computing power for planning, marketing, accounting, etc. as mainframes had for the functions they performed on behalf of *Fortune 500* companies only a few decades back. In fact, the systems are faster and more agile now – at a fraction of the cost. The personal computer has enabled boutique businesses to spring up, capable of delivering products and services tailored to the tastes of individual customers – all at reasonable prices. In the field of information technology, the cellular telephone is one of the chief assets of entrepreneurs constantly on the move to find new business. In addition, the Internet is already capable of putting anyone who bothers to set up a web site in touch with the rest of the world. In the area of energy, advances in solar power, fuel cells and small-scale generation equipment will allow a much higher degree of self-sufficiency among isolated communities. So goodbye to electricity pylons and telephone wires. A solar panel and a cellular phone will do, thank you very much.

In one way technology has fulfilled the vision of the 1960s. It has created a world permanently in surplus. Our lives are ruled by the economics of surplus, not by the economics of scarcity. This is in total contradiction to the prophecy of the British economist, Thomas Malthus, who thought the world would starve through lack of food. In his famous *Essay on the Principle of Population* written in 1798, he stated that populations increase in geometric ratio and food only in arithmetic ratio. Well, he was wrong. Food prices have dropped dramatically in the last 25 years because there's a constant surplus of it. What's more, this situation applies to any other commodity you care to name – cotton, oil, coal, steel, copper, nickel, aluminium, gold. In the manufacturing field, even if you write off the entire automobile production capacity of North America, you will still have surplus capacity elsewhere to meet the world's demand for cars. We have mastered the mass production technique to such an extent that there is very little value left in it. Customisation and the knowledge-intensive end of the production chain are where the value lies today. So poor people aren't poor because of scarcity of resources and products. Poor people are poor because they are denied the opportunity to make money for themselves. If they do, there's an endless supply of cheap goods to satisfy their demands.

Against this background, how do we reshape tomorrow's world of work to generate the kind of income which will take up the current slack in the market? How do we take the vast numbers of excluded, alienated people and give them a real sense of ownership in the economy? That is the challenge. For, without a short run, there can be no long run.

The sweet spot

In order to meet tomorrow's challenge, a "paradigm shift" is necessary. This is now a well-worn expression used by business gurus to describe a fundamental transformation in attitude or mindset. But what does it take to shift a person's paradigm? Barbara Tuchman in her book *The March of Folly* demonstrated just how much people stick to their opinions even when evidence is plainly pointing in another direction. The Trojans simply would not listen to Cassandra's warning that there were Greeks in the horse at their gates. The British couldn't believe that they would lose the American colonies. America couldn't contemplate withdrawal from Vietnam. Loss of face got in the way every time. So what makes the penny drop?

There are basically two methods – one brutal and one gentle. I am indebted to Richard Bolleurs, a Johannesburg businessman who knows a thing or two about the difficulty of changing a company's paradigm, for acquainting me with the first method. It is called the "Vesuvius model". In the spring of 79 AD, the Roman inhabitants of Pompeii, a sleepy city near the Bay of Naples, were not unduly concerned about the puffs of smoke emanating from Vesuvius.

Despite a rumble which caused some damage 16 years previously – a few statues fell, some columns were broken – the prevailing paradigm amongst the city folk was that the volcano was essentially harmless. So picture the local fishermen returning in their boats the morning after Vesuvius blew in the summer of 79. Imagine their faces as they surveyed the scene. The whole region was covered in molten lava, mud, ashes, cinders and stones. It must have been a terrifying sight and it certainly changed their opinion about the danger of Vesuvius.

The Vesuvius model explains why there has been such a paradigm shift on smoking (without, I may add, the need for legislation). People have examined the statistics on lung cancer and decided to stop. Excessive consumption of alcohol may be the next in line for becoming socially unacceptable. The Vesuvius model is also behind the behaviour of investors who sell at the bottom rather than at the top. Whilst the share price is rising, they're happy to hold on. When it drops, greed is replaced by terror which triggers a sale at precisely the wrong moment of the cycle. A sufficient degree of pain can turn a bull into a bear overnight. The East Rand gives us a similar insight into human fallibility. It was only when the gold mines closed that people woke up to the idea that gold was not forever and other industries had to be nurtured to replace it.

Sadly, the Vesuvius model may equally apply to the evolution of the HIV and AIDS epidemic. Two paradigms prevail. The first is that the spreading of the epidemic is as inevitable as the flooding of the plains downstream which follows the onset of the monsoon rains in the upper Ganges. Secondly, it is widely believed that the flood won't affect the people on the high ground – only those in the valley below. Both these propositions are false. In the first instance, we can make a difference because the transmission rate of the disease, i.e.

the number of people one person normally infects, is relatively low compared to, say, malaria or flu. Fatalism – a *que sera, sera* attitude to which a lot of us are prone – is entirely inappropriate in this case. The disease can be stopped in its tracks, given a national will to conquer it. Secondly, if we don't make a difference, the fury of the epidemic will affect everyone as our economy becomes increasingly unworkable with those of working age being hardest hit. However, it would appear that the full extent of the calamity will only be appreciated when a quarter of our population have been wiped out and the mortuaries can't cope with the thousands of young people dying daily on the streets. Only then will behaviour change. Meanwhile, AIDS is the biggest threat to South Africa's future – bar none.

Thus, a major discontinuity certainly shifts a paradigm. But why wait until a disaster strikes? Why allow necessity to be the mother of invention? These two questions form a perfect introduction to the other technique which was described by my scenario-planning mentor, Pierre Wack, as the "gentle art of re-perception". Indeed, this was the title of the avant-garde article he wrote in the *Harvard Business Review* in the mid-1980s. The art in question is to bring to the Emperor's attention that he has no clothes without him even knowing that you suggested it!

Pierre felt that there was something deeper and more subtle to scenario work than just outlining future possibilities. He maintained that nothing was more dangerous than a poorly observed fact. Witness Vesuvius! By looking at the present state of affairs from all sides and, in particular, by delving into those elements which were predetermined for all futures, we could narrow down the range of possibilities. This could lead to powerful new insights about the forces shaping the future and enable us to say: "Aha! This is really what is important and what is not." In consequence, we might be able to identify unusual points of leverage – areas where a limited effort could result in a major improvement.

To illustrate his point, Pierre loved telling the story of how, on a visit to Japan, he watched a gardener throwing pebbles at a bamboo trunk. When he asked the gardener why he was doing this, the gardener said that if the stone glanced off the trunk, the noise would be a dull thud. If, however, the stone hit the sweet spot in the middle, the sound would be a satisfying, resonant clonk. Moreover, the gardener added, if one focused one's mind in advance on imagining this distinctive sound, it improved the chances of hitting the sweet spot. Thereupon he picked up a pebble, went into a Zen-like trance and "clonked" the centre of the bamboo.

Let me give you a "clonk" which is thankfully academic to us but will not be so in a few million millennia. The laws of astronomy imply that our sun may eventually turn into a red giant and incinerate the Earth. Our future then narrows down to two options: face mass extinction or find another planet. This revelation should lead us to re-perceive the value of programmes to improve space travel and construct space stations.

But now for a famous example of re-perception actually hitting the sweet spot in 1543. In that year, the Polish astronomer, Nicolaus Copernicus, published his masterpiece, *Concerning the Revolutions of the Celestial Spheres*. In it, he refuted Ptolemy's theory that the Earth was the centre of the universe around which everything else revolved. Instead, Copernicus demonstrated how the Earth's motion could be used to explain the movements of other heavenly bodies. We do not sense the Earth hurtling through space because we are travelling with it. This simple re-perception opened the way for Johannes Kepler's laws of planetary motion, Isaac Newton's principle of gravitation and latterly Albert Einstein's general theory of relativity. The dam walls burst just as they did when it was recognised that the Earth was round, not flat.

Around 300 years after the discovery of a moving Earth, a young naturalist named Charles Darwin set sail on *HMS Beagle* to survey wildlife in South America and some Pacific Islands. From minutely studying all the specimens and fossils he collected, he gradually re-perceived the history of Earth in another dimension to that of Copernicus. He realised that we, and everything else in nature, had evolved according to the principle of natural selection (or survival of the fittest). The publishing of the book *On the Origin of Species* in 1859 was genuinely earth-shattering. Why? Because Darwin's theory contradicted the paradigm widely held at the time that the Earth was created literally in accordance with the story in the book of Genesis. Despite the initial controversy, most of us have managed to reconcile our religious beliefs with the idea that we are descended from primitive hominids. We have re-perceived our past. The latest find in the Sterkfontein Caves of the almost complete, fossilised remains of a man who lived three million years ago only serves to confirm that Darwin hit the sweet spot.

In 1986, the re-perception that was required in South Africa by the two principal opponents at the time – the National Party and the ANC – was that compromise through negotiation was preferable to a winner-takes-all philosophy. The "High Road" and "Low Road" scenarios were developed by our scenario team to promote this re-perception. They succeeded, and a civil war which would have suited nobody was averted. The parties were nudged to the table, whereafter good sense and a common South African-ness ensured a successful outcome. It proved that scenarios turn the unthinkable into the possible, the possible into the reasonable, and the reasonable into reality.

Now the crucial re-perception needed to consolidate our

future revolves around the changing nature of work, jobs and employment. In particular, we have to re-perceive the value of entrepreneurs, small business and the informal sector. We've done it once, so why can't we hit the sweet spot again? The first struggle was for everyone to be entitled to vote. The second struggle is for everyone to have economic liberty. It is just as noble a cause as the first one. And it requires just as much street-level activism. *A luta continua* in another context. I say this because I had breakfast a couple of years ago with an MK commander who'd exchanged his military fatigues for business civvies and had become the CEO of a parastatal. He felt lost in the business world which appeared bland in comparison to the former passion of the struggle when young people could be mobilised at the drop of a hat to do their duty. For him, something was missing. Well, it shouldn't be. The fight to give a better life to all is just as important and just as exciting as war.

Equally, we have another fight on our hands – against HIV and AIDS. If the virus were not microscopic and invisible but a human enemy threatening to invade our country and kill a quarter of our population, we would have re-mobilised the citizen force, bought tanks and fighter aircraft and gone into battle. We need to re-perceive the disease that way and use the weapons at our disposal. These include education on abstinence or protected sex (particularly sermons from the pulpit to show that the churches are fighting the good fight too); short courses of AZT – possibly in combination with 3TC – for pregnant mothers and newborn children which dramatically cut the probability of transmission; saturation media coverage; powerful new drugs already on the market to combat sexually transmitted diseases that facilitate the transmission of the virus; and the lobbying of universities and pharmaceutical companies to intensify their search for a cheap vaccine or cure. In addition, we should make it a serious crime for an HIV-positive person to pass on the virus knowingly to an unaware, non-HIV partner – particularly young girls where the rate of new infections is highest. The rights of non-HIVs have to be respected as much as HIVs. We have plenty of options in our arsenal to defeat the enemy. But we must be selective. There's no point in taking knives to a gunfight.

Hedgehogs and foxes

Fortunately, the key to solving the jobless problem also came to my ears in the 1960s. I was one of the privileged students in England to go to Oxford University. I did PPE – Politics, Philosophy and Economics – and majored in Philosophy. We had a philosopher there called Isaiah Berlin who talked of the difference between "hedgehogs" and "foxes" among the human population. He in turn had extracted this insight from fragments of a poem by an ancient Greek poet called Archilocus. How Archilocus arrived at this perception of the world remains, alas, unrecorded.

A hedgehog is a person who believes that life revolves around one big idea, one ultimate truth. If only we can get at that idea or truth, everything else will come right. Plato, the Greek philosopher, was a hedgehog because he was convinced that the world we are in is a mere shadow cast by the Real World behind it. Reasoning is the one faculty we possess to pierce the shadow and see the light. If you were in the fortunate position of being a really brilliant philosopher (like he was), you could do it. To this day, many politicians hold a similar opinion. If they can only discover the right ideology which will lead us all to the Real World, we will end up in Utopia. To whit, Karl Marx was an archetypal hedgehog with his ideology of Communism. But closely following in his footsteps are the miniature hedgehogs who congregate at Davos in Switzerland once a year and call for a New World Order or advocate a Third Way. It's all part of the hedgehog conspiracy to keep coming up with vague new formulae which ensure their continuing pre-eminence in world affairs! But the validity of these formulae is shorter-lived than that of an equation like $E = mc^2$. Add to this the plethora of 24-hour news networks which feature an endless number of blow-dried hedgehogs pontificating on this or that issue, as if the Real World is the one on the box, and you'll begin to catch my drift.

The latest example of hedgehog thinking is the way many people viewed the job summit that was held last year in South Africa. They believe that it only needs big government, big business and big labour to meet to produce a big rabbit out of a big hat. That will solve all the unemployment problems here. Of course, this is untrue: big government and big business are not going to be net job creators over the first part of the new century and the unions have never been in the business of creating jobs. QED, there are no rabbits in the hat. We shall have to look elsewhere for solutions; and, consequently, we should have a follow-up interchange which this time includes the entrepreneurs as key contributors. The objective would be to forge a partnership between the parties with the express intention of fostering small enterprise and overcoming the general aversion for investment in small business in this country. Moreover, the script should not be written beforehand. The dialogue of this summit, which I would like to call an enterprise summit, ought to be open and spontaneous.

A fox, in contrast to a hedgehog, is someone who believes that life is about knowing many things. Even then, it is at best confusing. The real world is the world we see – take it or leave it with all its imperfections. Aristotle, who was 37 when Plato died in 347 BC, was a fox. He proposed that experience was the source of all knowledge. For example, he thought that heavy objects fall faster than light objects. It was Galileo who two thousand years later refuted this with his discovery that freely falling bodies, heavy or light, have the same constant acceleration. Aristotle wouldn't have minded being proved wrong because to him the ultimate arbiter was experience.

William Shakespeare was a fox in that he exposed the frailties of kings and queens, together with their messy relationships, in his plays. Even at the level of royalty, he demonstrated that nothing was that simple. And this was long before Bill Clinton and Prince Charles were born! Adam Smith was a fox in that he wrote of the wealth of nations emanating from the invisible hand of the market. He inferred that whenever hedgehogs interfered, wealth was diminished. It may sound odd, but I would certainly classify John Maynard Keynes as a fox. He once chided his critics with these famous words: "When the facts change, I change my mind. What do you do, Sir?" If he were alive today, he would have looked at governments running permanent budget deficits in a bid to boost their economies and come to the conclusion that this kind of fix no longer served its purpose. He would probably advocate microeconomic reform like more flexible labour markets. Ironically, another famous quip of his was that most politicians are "slaves of some defunct economist". It's a pity that some of his devotees still mistake his recommendations for the 1930s as dogma for the 1990s. Keynes was a fox in another respect too. Short-term results mattered to him because "in the long run we are all dead". Hedgehogs so often excuse a disappointing performance in the short term on the grounds that the only worthwhile judgement is one taken over a long period of time. The question is: how long is long?

Karl Popper, another intellectual giant of the 20th century, was an Austrian fox. He believed that a scientific hypothesis could never be conclusively proved – only disproved. Hence, if over time nobody managed to falsify a hypothesis, then maybe it was true. Yet you could never be sure: look how long Aristotle's hypothesis for falling objects lasted. Popper's conclusion is very foxy, for it neatly illustrates the difference between the outlooks of foxes and hedgehogs. Foxes take after quantum physicists who accept that the future is driven by the principle of uncertainty, and there'll always be things we don't know and can't control. They take each day as it comes – hence the title of this book. They set modest goals, roll up their own sleeves and get their own hands dirty in achieving them. They regularly take bites out of the "reality sandwich" to keep their feet on the ground. They therefore have a healthy scepticism of grand visions which portray the world as a highly mechanistic and predictable system. Hedgehogs, on the other hand, maintain that if you're not in control, things are out of control. Hence, the aim must be to eliminate uncertainty, take charge and get other people to do the dirty work. John Lennon would have entirely disagreed with this sentiment. In his last album, *Double Fantasy*, he gave this advice to his son, Sean, in the song "Beautiful Boy": "Life is what happens to you while you're busy making other plans." Indeed, foxes understand that life consists of a series of unexpected forks in the road ahead. You'll never know whether you took the best turning because you'll never know what it would have been like to take the other one.

Consequently, a fox's ambition is limited to getting the majority of little things right, and then the big picture will automatically improve. Even though some little things will contradict other little things and sometimes some of the little things will be plain wrong, as long as the bulk of little things are moving society in the correct direction this is the best we can hope for. Think of how many wrong pieces we choose when we do a jigsaw puzzle before we select the right piece to insert. But life is more complicated than a puzzle, for its pieces are a mixture of opposites which require pragmatic blending and optimisation. For example, more equality means less freedom, more justice means less mercy. So it's all about finding a desirable balance.

One of the best scenes in any business video that I've watched is of Joel Barker walking down a beach and encountering a young boy throwing starfish into the sea. "Why are you doing this," Joel asks, "when so many are stranded on the shore?" The boy foxily replies: "See this particular starfish I'm holding in my hand? I'm changing its life." Every single little action counts, even if it means rescuing one starfish at a time. If we adopted this one-on-one philosophy in our schools and hospitals, the quality of delivery would improve immeasurably overnight.

Peter Senge, an American academic, was a fox after my own heart when he wrote *The Fifth Discipline*. He quoted the wonderful example of the beer game his business students played. No matter how clever they were, they always ended up with a vast surplus of beer to sell because they never figured out all the interdependencies in the system which got the beer to the customer. The game had in fact been rigged to produce this result! But this is precisely the trap that hedgehogs fall into time and again. By pursuing a big idea in a blinkered manner to the exclusion of everything else, they often end up by making the situation worse than before. Imagine what would happen if you introduced a million elephants into the Kruger Park because you had a passion for elephants. It would upset the ecosystem completely. In pursuit of some spurious ideology or idea they're fixated on, hedgehogs often do something similar. In relation to the main topic of this book, they don't realise that grand employment initiatives always have an opportunity cost attached to them. Whatever money is put into them has to come from somewhere else where jobs may have been created just as – if not more – efficiently. Moreover, there's always an element of "transmission loss" because of money being absorbed by administrative overheads, mainly comprising the salaries of the hedgehogs who have been appointed to dispense the largesse. Hedgehog-minded editors compound the felony by headlining the direct benefits of the proposed "scheme" in their newspapers. "New Plan for Jobs" they proclaim, but they never mention the indirect trade-offs!

Foxes have the slogan "ready, fire, aim", as they are only interested in action and results. If they fail the first time, they treat the failure as part of the learning curve on the journey to success. Failure does not mean wrong: it means try again. In contrast, hedgehogs have the slogan, "ready, aim, have a workshop, aim, have a conference, aim, have a summit, aim and, if all else fails, set up a commission, aim . . ." They never pull the trigger and fire, as they are so busy searching for that one perfect idea; and they honestly feel that talk is progress. Hence, they love participating in chat shows. One hedgehog I know, when asked to be on a panel, declined with the memorable line that Pavarotti does not sing in a choir! He wanted to be the centre of attention on the programme. For all their blah, hedgehogs fail to put their money where their mouths are. They hate grasping nettles, taking tough decisions and firing other incompetent hedgehogs. In the case of foxes, action speaks louder than words.

A neat illustration of the difference between the two species is highlighted by the issue of emigration. Hedgehogs will agonise for years over whether to stay or leave South Africa to the extent that they remain in a permanent state of suspended animation. In spirit, they hibernate, because they're always going to leave next year. Foxes, on the other hand, either make a full-blooded commitment to this country or get on the next flight out. They don't sit around and whinge. More to the point, they treat it as a matter of no great principle either way. It's for each individual to decide, in his or her own circumstances, where it's best to live. Unfortunately, violent crime is tipping the balance in favour of a job overseas for many young professionals.

Being a fox or a hedgehog is all about mindset, whether you work in large or small business, the private or public sector. In other words, besides foxy entrepreneurs, you can have foxy politicians, foxy directors-general and foxy teachers. Foxes have the philosophy that you only get anywhere by dint of your own efforts. Hedgehogs assume that the world owes them a living. Foxes deal in specifics whereas hedgehogs make speeches full of motherhood and apple pie statements. In the cut and thrust of arguments, foxes play the ball and address the issue; hedgehogs play the person and place undue emphasis on his or her background and credentials. If you belong to the wrong side, you've got no chance of being heard by a hedgehog. If you're on the same side, you can get away with almost anything because hedgehogs protect their own.

Commercial foxes believe there are only two seasons: slack and busy. Hedgehogs never return telephone calls because they are always too busy. They regard their time as far more valuable than yours so they'll keep you waiting just for the pleasure of it. Foxes naturally believe in decentralisation of power and letting people do their own thing. Hedgehogs are natural centralisers since they think they know best and like to feel that society depends on their superior intellect. Whilst trumpeting slogans like "up the workers", hedgehogs secretly would prefer the proletariat to remain dumbed down and therefore in need of somebody to look up to and worship. Hedgehogs are particularly wicked when it comes to creating a dependency culture amongst minority groups. They hand out the welfare and the whisky to indigenous minorities such as American Indians, Eskimos and Aborigines whilst making no attempt at integrating them into the mainstream society. Their policy is: keep them stoned and at a distance in some location or other. It's separate development with a vengeance. Foxes like to operate in a no-holds-barred free-enterprise system where the colour of money is more important than the colour of skin. Hedgehogs are more comfortable with crony capitalism where they can pull the strings and give special deals to their friends.

Foxes regard a diversity of opinion as a cornerstone of a healthy society. Hedgehogs preach unity – on their own terms of course! Intimidation and exerting pressure to conform to their point of view are the stock in trade of hedgehogs. If you're not for them, you're against them. They can dish out sarcasm and criticism but don't like being on the receiving end of either. Fortunately, foxes are pretty thick-skinned in the face of criticism from hedgehogs and will not allow it to divert them from their objective. Hedgehogs join bandwagons; foxes love underdogs and minority opinions. Hence, trade unionists don't like foxes that much. They aren't good membership material as they don't have a sufficiently collectivist outlook. To a cunning member of the fox species, an injury to one is an opportunity for someone else! You'll find plenty of these opportunistic foxes sitting on the reserve benches at soccer, cricket and rugby matches.

Foxes and hedgehogs have a natural dislike for each other because foxes regard themselves as sovereign individuals (and in groups sovereign companies), whereas hedgehogs are always trying to control the foxes. Foxes want to own things; hedgehogs want to own people. Foxes rely on trust and a handshake; hedgehogs bring lawyers and agreements to sign. Hedgehogs legislate for anything that moves because "there ought to be a law against it" and they know what's good for you; foxes prefer social pressures to change all but the most obnoxious behaviour. Hedgehogs seek to impose their will, no matter what, although they may indulge in some phoney consultation beforehand. They're used to a labour-driven economy where management and workers deal with each other collectively in a confrontational mode. Foxes presume that we've moved to a more individualistic society where the sharing of knowledge is the key to consensus. They therefore prefer the strategies of persuasion and participation to get those around them to buy into their ideas. The European Union is a litmus test for differentiating foxes from hedgehogs. The former view it primarily as an economic union in which foxes of different nationalities can freely trade with one another. The latter see it primarily as a political union which expands control by the Brussels hedgehogs over member states. It's all a matter of voluntary co-operation versus compulsory obedience. At the moment, the hedgehogs are winning.

Hedgehogs cannot understand how anybody can work for himself or herself. They regard the small business sector as a refugee camp for those who have failed to find conventional jobs. Foxes regard small business as their natural habitat. They don't mind at all being excluded from the national GDP statistics. They stand less chance of detection by overzealous and bureaucratic gamekeepers intent on making them pay tax. Hedgehog municipalities banish hawkers from town centres to remote sites where pedestrian traffic is minimal. Foxy municipalities make the hawkers pay for prime pavement space, and regulate the numbers that way. Hedgehogs like to announce large new projects where the workers salute the rulers as they used to do in those old Communist propaganda posters. Never mind that the projects turn into white elephants because the output can't be disposed of at economic prices or that they drain the national economy of capital. Hedgehogs are marking the coming millennium with monuments costing stupendous sums of money. Foxes shrug their shoulders and say: "So what about 2000 – it's an artificial date anyway."

Generally speaking, hedgehog economies rely too much on single commodities and mass production. They belong to the Stone Age. Foxy economies are diversified (though each fox is focused) and transform themselves as new industries replace old industries. Like nature, the sheer variety of species make foxy economies more resilient to changes in the economic environment. America gets more than half its economic growth from industries established in the last ten years. I was asked a marvellous question the other day: "Which grossed more in Britain in 1997? Shipping, steel and coal combined or oriental restaurants?" The answer is oriental restaurants because there are eight thousand of them. Hedgehog-leaning economists imply that economies are driven by balance-of-payments considerations, interest rates and money supply. Foxy economists know that economies are driven by flesh-and-blood individuals who produce and consume (which is why HIV/AIDS will have a delayed but devastating impact on the economy if allowed to spread unchecked).

Hedgehogs love attending international conferences on aid and development. They are the "lords of poverty". In fact, there's a "five-star" subspecies of hedgehog who obviously is not aware that you can communicate internationally by telephone. At the hint of a lunch invitation, he travels first class overseas – with aides in tow – to have a face-to-face discussion with the person he could have phoned or emailed. Foxes prefer to stay at home and concentrate on the fine tuning of developmental policies to create the optimum environment for other foxes to thrive. Hedgehogs portray immigrants as people who displace locals from jobs. Foxes regard immigrants as an addition to their pool of talent which will lead to the further creation of jobs. In the same vein, hedgehogs positively discourage foreign investment by hedging it about with all kinds of conditions. Foxes understand that you have to lay out a welcoming mat to induce foreigners to take the risk of entering your home. They widely advertise that the country is open for business. They see the collapse of the Far East as an ideal opportunity of attracting much needed foreign capital to South Africa. They dream that we could become the premier emerging market in the eyes of Wall Street and London. Hedgehogs stoop to economic policies of protection when the going gets tough. Foxes recognise that protection is a formula for inefficiency and anyway runs the danger of a tit-for-tat response from foreign trading partners.

Hedgehogs believe that problems can be fixed by throwing money at them. They tend to select complicated, costly, First World solutions with no thought for the quality and quantity of manpower necessary to implement them. Foxes know that throwing good money after bad achieves nothing. Things get done because of highly committed individuals. Foxes therefore mould organisations and solutions around the people they've got. Hedgehogs pigeonhole people into preordained structures. Foxes know that organisational mergers often produce a clash of cultures and personalities because it's a collection of individual souls that you're merging. Hedgehogs move people around like pieces on a chessboard, preferring to concentrate on the overall rationale of the game rather than the human consequences. Hedgehogs also build large, uniform housing estates where every house is the same. Foxes prefer villages which grow in a topsy-turvy fashion and cater for the individual needs of the villagers. In order of precedence, foxes put their family and friends ahead of their career or cause. Hedgehogs do quite the reverse – the Cause swallows them up. Hedgehog parents neglect their children; foxy mothers and fathers juggle their diaries.

Foxes invite criticism; hedgehogs crave flattery. Hedgehogs are legends in their own mind and therefore surround themselves with yes-men. Foxes know their weaknesses and choose colleagues who have strengths to complement their weaknesses. You may have bumped into hypocritical hedgehogs. They're the ones who expect everyone else to do as they say even as they do the exact opposite. They believe they're so big, they can play by their own rules. Foxes, on the whole, inspire people by setting an example. Hedgehogs speak in slow, measured tones with long pauses to underline the seriousness of what they're saying. They waste their energy dreaming up new terminology and hyphenated buzz words that confuse everyone. Foxes spontaneously speak their minds and often meet themselves coming the other way in an argument because they see both points of view. Hedgehogs sound like "Bolero" – one note repeated again and again. Foxes come across like a good jazz band – a mixture of structure and improvisation.

As far as innovation is concerned, foxes dream of what can be while hedgehogs find it easier to say no. Foxes challenge the status quo; hedgehogs stick to it. Foxes are outsiders with inner conviction. Hedgehogs are insiders with outer bravado. Martin Luther was a fox when he wrote an attack on the sale of indulgences which he nailed to a church door on October 31, 1517. Princess Diana was a fox in that she single-handedly changed the rules governing the interaction between the Royal Family and the public.

he has furnished with a cellular phone and lap-top computer. He spends his life on the road visiting the operations. Another CEO uses the local coffee shop as his headquarters. In return for providing the shop with a regular clientele, he gets a table free to use as a desk with the waitress doubling as his office assistant. Closer to home, Laurie Dippenaar won the 1998 *Sunday Times* businessman-of-the-year award as the foxy CEO of First Rand, the largest banking group in South Africa. He comes from a long pedigree of foxes in Rand Merchant Bank. He maintains that the modern corporate model is a federation of "states". The function of the centre is to ensure the presence of a free-market and moral ethic throughout the group. The only way you know whether a central service department is offering something genuinely of value to the subsidiary companies is to give them the opportunity of turning it down – either because they don't want it at all or because they can get it cheaper elsewhere. Thus a foxy leader ensures that tight loops of accountability exist in his organisation through voluntary choice and competition rather than commands from "on high".

The restructuring of one head office and one university I know has resulted in many foxes coming out of the woodwork. Their departments have been converted into stand-alone companies which market themselves not only to their traditional in-house clients but to other outside customers as well. Each of the two institutions has commercialised its centres of excellence and thereby dropped its overhead cost. In contrast, hedgehogs build high-rise Kremlins from which they can run their domains like sovereigns and impose their uncalled-for services on minions who are obliged to pay.

In the political sphere, hedgehogs rely on rhetoric all the time; foxes campaign in poetry and govern in prose. A foxy government is one which focuses on doing only those things that the private sector can't do. Obviously, a government must tax the better-off individuals and companies to finance the provision of services to the poor. The private sector can't tax itself! But the actual delivery of virtually every service you care to mention – health, education, transport, mail, water, electricity, road construction and maintenance, telecommunication, rubbish collection, sewage disposal, etc. – can be done by private foxes in competition with one another.

The only functions that need to be retained as direct arms of the government are finance, law and order, home affairs, foreign affairs and defence. The rest of the ministries could be subsumed in these.

Alas, despite privatisation, hedgehog-type governments still abound in the world, trying to duplicate what the private sector can do better. Worse still, plenty of state hedgehogs sit at their desks all day long twiddling their thumbs as there is no money for them to do anything except be paid a salary. The salary bill has crowded out all other items of government expenditure. Hedgehogs look after their own, even if they're crooked, until the last possible moment. This occurs when foxes stop voting for them or stop paying taxes because they see nothing in return. Hedgehogs extol transparency until there is something awkward that they have to be transparent about. Then they curl up into little balls and become very prickly and obscure. Foxes see through that ploy. Africa used to be foxy before the Europeans arrived. Each village was a tightly knit community in which everyone from the chief down had a distinctive and meaningful role to play. The Europeans arbitrarily divided Africa up into nation-states, each with a huge administrative apparatus of hedgehogs. Down the years, the legacy has survived with each new cadre of hedgehogs sucking the lifeblood out of their respective economies. As a way of buttressing their

not a right to a job, or the right to earn a salary any more; but the right to make a living, to carve out a livelihood. Notice the move from passive to active citizenship, from slave to master of your own destiny. And that goes for South Africa as much as it does for any other country. It also explains the burgeoning popularity of self-help books and courses. People are tumbling to the new reality that creating a job is, to put it mildly, nonsensical without a commercial opportunity to precede it. Rather than "back to the future", we are fast-forwarding into the past. We are going back to the days before the growth of the great bureaucracies, to the time when florins changed hands for genuinely added value or "real work".

This brings me to the final distinction between hedgehogs and foxes. It concerns affirmative action. Hedgehogs use the phrase in the narrow sense of creating a mixed hedgehog universe from which foxes remain excluded (as they always were in the past). The broader definition of affirmative action means a rising tide of prosperity which lifts all the little boats in the harbour as well as the cruise ships! Everybody benefits – foxes and hedgehogs alike. I can't tell you how important this is because, as of now, the majority of foxes in this country believe that the economy is owned by "them" – white and black hedgehogs who've made it through contacts, not merit. I won't start believing that we've aspired to a properly mixed universe until I walk into a pizzeria or deli in Sandton City where the black owner greets me at the door.

In Jamaica, religious leaders talk of the Mustard Seed Model, but it's the same principle that I've just been advocating. The reference to mustard comes from the Bible: "Despise not the days of small beginnings ... The kingdom of heaven is like to a grain of mustard seed, which a man took, and sowed in his field: which indeed is the least of all seeds: but when it is grown, it is the greatest among herbs, and becometh a tree, so that the birds of the air come and lodge in the branches thereof." Foxes believe in small beginnings – plenty of them.

Capital for foxes

How do we go about constructing a system that not only permits but positively encourages poverty-stricken communities to dig themselves out of the poverty trap? Put another way, how do we establish an environment in South Africa which is friendly to foxes, an environment that positively draws them out of their foxholes? The Grand Fox of them all, Don MacRobert, who used to run the Get Ahead Foundation, which has assisted tens of thousands of South African entrepreneurs since its inception, mentions one word: credit. The first aspect of a fox-friendly environment has therefore to do with money. Money really does make the world go round. Capitalism was called capitalism for a good reason. Without capital, foxes can only dream. They can never turn their dreams into business realities.

Incidentally, this statement applies equally to the social entrepreneurs, i.e. the foxes who run the nongovernmental organisations (NGOs) and who have to be especially entrepreneurial in fund-raising. This last talent is essential when big charity drives such as national lotteries are hoovering up the bulk of a nation's social spending. Hedgehogs who predominate on the boards of these grand charities tend to give the money away to other hedgehogs, leaving little or none for the foxes. Social entrepreneurs are also wary of smooth hedgehogs who are all sweet-talk when it comes to moral support for projects, but never inject a cent themselves. Yet, many foxy NGOs are incredible job-creating

because you are perceived to be too bad a risk. It's one of those quirky laws of banking that if you want a R5 million loan you'll get it; but if you want R5 000 you won't. The advertisement showing a panel of three bank managers climbing over the desk clamouring "please don't go" to a potential client does not apply to the township fox. A bemused look is more like it, together with the question: "Are you lost or something? Please go." The circle is vicious because if you haven't got money as security, you can't get money. In fact, in South Africa it's easier to get credit for consumption than for production; anyone can open an account at a clothing store. Foxes cannot survive in such a situation.

The remedy is to do what California did in the early 1990s. Faced with the loss of half a million jobs in the defence industry there, caused by Pentagon cutbacks following the collapse of the Soviet Union, the Californian state government immediately instituted a credit guarantee scheme for loans to small business. They also got the major banks to come to the party. As a result, small business boomed; and not only were the half million jobs recovered, another half million jobs were added as well.

California, by itself, is now the seventh largest economy in the world with only 32 million people. The ranking goes: America, Japan, Germany; then in a bunch France, Britain, Italy; then California. Thus, California is the foxiest state around. Its renaissance was entirely due to the fact that they went gung-ho on small business formation – not just in high-technology industries in Silicon Valley but in humdrum activities such as furniture and toy manufacture, restaurants, video hire ships, laundromats. Come to think of it, just the kind of businesses that already exist in any town you visit in South Africa. Even Hollywood is now a cluster of small businesses, each with its own speciality.

Movies today are temporary alliances between these specialists. The big old studios have virtually all gone. For example, the majority of the companies involved in the making of *Titanic* had less than 30 employees. The wider figure for the Californian economy is that 80 per cent of Californians work in businesses of less than 200 people.

Amazingly, California is a semi-arid state like South Africa. Water is as precious as gold. With the San Andreas fault running slap through it, California suffers the additional handicap of experiencing the occasional major earthquake. Furthermore, Californians have limited natural resources after the "forty-niners" extracted most of the gold 150 years ago. This is probably a blessing in disguise, since they haven't contracted the "oil disease", i.e. too much of a dependency on a single commodity. So where does their success come from? It began with the raw energy of the initial immigrants who were the American equivalent of the Voortrekkers when they struck out west. This fine, pioneering tradition was carried forward by the new immigrants who have turned California into one of the most mixed, exciting and venturesome societies on Earth. Californians are foxes of all stripes – with attitude. They even have the sparkle to say: "The San Andreas is not my fault." There's nothing to stop us having the same sparkle and boldness here.

In South Africa, the Ministry of Trade and Industry has recently launched a company called Khula (which in Xhosa means "to grow"). It is currently capitalised at a little over R300 million, but it is hoped to boost this figure to R500 million at the beginning of the new century. Khula is fantastic. It's the ace in the government's pack. It lends money to specialist retail institutions that onlend it to the foxes. But, just as crucial in the longer term, it plays a role in providing credit guarantees to entrepreneurs. The Khula process works

Americans have discovered that the nature of risk is changing. Specifically, the risk/reward ratios for small, highly focused businesses in fast-growing market niches are often more favourable than for bigger companies subject to the broader cycles of the world economy. Hence, pension funds are allocating up to five per cent of their portfolios for investment in small businesses. It should be emphasised that they are not doing this for reasons of social responsibility but because it is financially sensible to do so. The average return on venture capital in the United States at the moment lies between 30 and 40 per cent per annum. On top of this, bigger is no longer necessarily safer these days. Smaller can be a better bet. Japan offers a sobering experience of how risk has changed. The banks there have racked up bad debts of over half a trillion dollars on large projects. Perhaps they should have put more effort into backing the small Japanese foxes. It would have been a more responsible strategy in retrospect – for depositors and shareholders alike.

An alternative way of skinning the equity cat is to interpose intermediaries between financial institutions and the small and microbusinesses who need the capital. What I'm thinking of is the formation of investment trusts which specialise in venture capital activities and have a portfolio of interests in foxy companies to reduce the risk. These umbrella entities could be quoted on the JSE (or Sasdaq). California has 2 500 venture capital companies doing such work. Old Mutual will not invest in a single spaza shop; but it might be willing to invest in the Khayelitsha Investment Trust run by a competent fund manager. With a greater proportion of personal savings flowing into mutual funds every year, this has to be an avenue to explore. One could even think of turning stokvels, which are already an important source of income in the townships, into investment trusts.

Another halfway house is to set up a market site on the

Internet. On this site, foxes could advertise that they are seeking capital for certain types of business and venture capitalists could identify the lines of businesses they want to put their money into. This kind of matchmaking site is already up and running in Australia. Here, EDS Africa has launched a web site called *www.smme.co.za* to provide a database for small business. The JSE also intends to set up a web site called *www.eez.co.za* that will match national and international capital providers with local small-business-capital seekers. By the way, "eez" stands for "emerging enterprise zone".

One criticism of all these schemes is that looser regulations will inevitably imply a greater number of scams and frauds. Alas, it was ever thus. "Caveat emptor" or "buyer beware" has always been the best principle to govern a market. It is certainly a lot better than copious regulations which stifle any form of entrepreneurial activity. Anyway, remember that no accounting firms were around to audit the books of the companies first floated on the JSE during the gold rush. Yet it worked! The gold prospectors got their money from strangers to dig their claims. Their prospectuses were simple: if we hit gold, you'll be worth a fortune; if we don't hit gold, you lose your investment. Period. And it opened the way for the biggest economic boom in South Africa's history. So, to avoid being taken to the cleaners like the British investors who were sold prime real estate in the Louisiana swamps, the best thing is to go and see a prospective investment for yourself. Proximity is an important consideration when deciding where to put your venture capital.

In South Africa, we're obsessed with building casinos. All that's going to happen is that the savings of the masses will end up in the pockets of a few casino owners. Casinos are programmed for people to lose and 70 per cent of their prof-

remaining weapons into the river. The risk of continuing to have an unlicenced firearm outweighed the risk of not having one. How is that known? Because the rivers dried up not so long ago and there were the guns rusting on the riverbeds. Meanwhile, an international study recently came to the conclusion that the proliferation of small arms now poses a greater threat to global society than nuclear weapons. The gun manufacturers have a lot to answer for. Indeed, guns are worse than drugs because they are more harmful to other people's health. Their purpose is to kill. Somehow, the citizens of this world are going to have to create a gun-free society.

In South Africa, we're trying to curb cigarettes, not guns (although recent reports that the government is finally going to crack down on the latter are heartening). Consequently, the prevailing paradigm is that crime is unstoppable and can only get worse. A young police reservist remarked to me that this must be the only country where, in a collision between two cars, everybody at the scene is armed – the drivers, the police, the traffic police, the witnesses, the paramedics and the tow-truck drivers (all legally). It's as bad as Dodge City before such famous peacemakers as Wyatt Earp and Bat Masterson enforced the law and cleaned up the place. Its city hall now stands on Boot Hill, so named because many gunmen in the 1870s were buried there, still wearing their boots.

A victim of gangsters came to one of my presentations a few weeks ago in Johannesburg. She operates a small classroom in Soweto which she stocks with second-hand personal computers using 386 or 486 microprocessors. She loads them with maths and English language programmes and the students pay a small fee for the extra tuition offered by these programmes. Three times she has been cleaned out by the township gangsters. She says to me: "How can I be a fox when the Tsotsies come and destroy my business?" Lesotho is the ultimate example of how destructive crime can be for foxes. One day of madness occurred in Maseru in 1998 when virtually every shop was looted or burnt to the ground. It undid fifty years of economic progress in 24 hours. Whatever quantity of aid is pumped in to restore the situation, it will not persuade the foxes to return in a hurry and risk their necks again.

Law and order is vital for another reason. Young people must have foxes to look up to, and not succumb to the idea that the gangsters, who are nothing but wolves, should be their role models. But the latter will happen if the gangsters are the only rich people around. I was talking at the annual banquet of the Cape Town City Mission just recently. They do fantastic work among the street children in Mitchell's Plain. Nevertheless, they were bemoaning the fact that the youngsters on the Cape Flats see the gangsters as heroes. After all, they're the guys who drive the BMWs and have gold chains around their necks. Most of the crime in this country is attributable to small packs of highly professional wolves. They must be trapped and put away in cages for a long time. With only one in seven reported murders and one in 50 reported hijackings ending in conviction, the police and the courts have a long way to go in rounding up the wolves in the forest.

In the longer run, if we don't do something now, we could end up like some South American countries where the wolves behave like the one who accosted Little Red Riding Hood in the forest. "What big pockets you have!" say the family in the slums. "All the better to give you another school or hospital," the wolf replies. "But that's for the government to do," continue the family. "Don't worry," declares the wolf with a contented burp, which always follows a good meal, "be happy that they no longer exist.

try again. They don't want to become mired up in red tape manufactured by bureaucratic hedgehogs bristling with importance. In South Africa, the number of permits to open up a small business legitimately is mind-boggling. As one fox put it, you have to cut the red tape longways to get anywhere in South Africa! A Dutch fox who runs a guesthouse in Somerset West describes it another way: "My experience of setting up a business here reminds me of a saying in Holland which, basically translated, highlights the difficulty of using a garden hose to water against the wind." Hence, many township businesses operate outside the law. It is essential to simplify the system whereby a fox can set up a business. Uganda again leads the way. You can get all the permits you require to become an entrepreneur at a one-stop agency in Kampala – and that applies to foreigners as well as locals.

On a different front, we had a poverty summit recently in South Africa where the opinions of poverty-stricken people were heard on how to beat the poverty trap. Again and again, the opinion was expressed that one of the main restrictions stopping women from becoming entrepreneurs in the rural areas was the traditional structures of authority. Women were not allowed to own land, women were discouraged from any form of cash-generating enterprise, etc. Yet around the world the new entrepreneurial wave is being led by women since they have an uncanny ability to spot the gaps in the market and then form a close relationship with their customer base. Surveys in England and America have shown that small businesses run by women have a much greater chance of survival than those run by men. In Bangladesh, 93 per cent of the borrowers from the Grameen Bank which specialises in loans to microenterprises are women. This initiative is turning their society upside down.

So don't forget the foxy ladies of South Africa. They are part of the new wave.

You have to ask yourself why Indians outside of India, Pakistanis outside Pakistan, Chinese outside of China and Jews outside of Israel are such successful foxes. For example, the 18 million Indians living outside India are collectively responsible for a greater GDP than the 939 million living inside India. Part of the reason may be that emigrants tend to be the pioneering sort; but distance from the suffocating influence of the hedgehogs in their home countries surely plays a role too. Foxes out of captivity are more resilient than foxes in a zoo. They have more self-confidence to follow their own trail. America, in a sense, is a gigantic melting pot of immigrants. It must be one of the reasons they've done so well, because each new immigrant sheds the baggage of history and class when he or she draws breath for the first time on America's soil (just like I did when I came to South Africa from England).

In a funny way, the end of Apartheid meant freedom for the Afrikaners as well as for black people. Up till 1994, 60 per cent of Afrikaners were in state employment of one kind or another. Many were perfect hedgehog stereotypes. Now the doors of the civil service are closed, they have to be foxes. But, like trapeze artists, they have discovered to their surprise that they perform better without safety nets. Just go to the University of Pretoria and see the fundamental change in attitude of the students there. In marked contrast to the previous slave-like mentality of deciding which government department or parastatal organisation to join, they are looking to do their own thing. And the sky's the limit. Moreover, the university established the first Chair of Entrepreneurship in South Africa. We can safely say that, in developing a foxy society, Pretoria leads the way!

There is one other prerequisite for freedom which I have

exchange. If corporate taxes remain unchanged, foxes will not come out of their foxholes to list their companies. They will not risk paying tax because of the additional transparency associated with a publicly quoted company. If you want foxes to come out into the open, don't penalise them with excessive tax rates. Reduce them to an appropriate level and grant tax holidays up to a certain point.

Education for foxes

Many members of audiences I address on entrepreneurship ask me whether you are born an entrepreneur or whether you can be trained to be an entrepreneur. The answer most definitely is the latter. Entrepreneurs aren't rocket scientists. Anyone can open a small business, should they put their mind to it. But the last part of the previous sentence is an important qualification. Schools still teach children as if they are about to join a hedgehog society where everything is scheduled and certain, and loyalty and passivity are rewarded. Originality which makes a child stray outside the standard curriculum is frowned upon. The basic educational paradigm is: hard work and good grades will be rewarded by a nice nine-to-five career, five days a week for 40 years. Then you retire on a pension and then you die. I recall a classic folk song by Pete Seeger about suburban homes that he likened to little boxes "all made out of ticky-tacky and they all look just the same".

Pleasantville, a recently released movie, explores the same concept, although it's mainly in monochrome due to an ingenious plot. The film is about an immaculate US suburb in the 1950s where everybody conforms so much to accepted values and customs that they lead colourless lives. Only when kids from the 1990s go back in time and invade the suburb do splashes of colour appear. Anybody who is persuaded to deviate from the norm is betrayed by colour. Well, we have a whiff of Pleasantville in our education system. In essence, our children are trained to be followers (and employees) rather than foxes (and owners). Alas, therefore, many good schools – and universities for that matter – are brilliantly educating their pupils for the job market of the 1950s. They haven't woken up to the fact that the nature of work in the outside world has undergone a sea change. You create a job now by identifying a niche rather than seeking a job that already exists. Even as parents, we fall into the trap of instilling a culture of dependency in our children. We behave like the welfare state when we give them pocket money. We ought rather to adopt a policy of helping them to help themselves.

However, I'm glad to say that a few schools in South Africa are breaking the mould, including a marvellous one in Pietermaritzburg called The Wykeham Collegiate whose motto is: "Educating women for the real world". The school starts by teaching girls as young as eight to play business games. Then they graduate to selling crisps, soft drinks and other provisions on school property. Then they begin manufacturing items such as plastic jewellery and personalised key rings that they sell to the public at open days on school grounds. One girl recently received an order for 16 000 key rings from a company in Pietermaritzburg; so her parents are going to work at weekends in the foreseeable future! Finally, when they are in senior school, the girls submit business plans to the school's chamber of commerce. If the plans are approved, they obtain real loans from real banks in Pietermaritzburg. Should they go bust, real dads bail them out. Nonetheless, some of them are earning as much as the teachers and one or two have parents who've taken time-out from their regular occupations

perform better than half-hearted bureaucrats going through the motion for their monthly salaries. I call the latter cheque collectors. In particular, the centres should be staffed by the old foxes, i.e. people retired or semiretired from owning and operating little businesses. Grey power needs to be harnessed as business angels. Who better to watch over the young entrepreneurs?

I've always said that joblessness is more fundamental than homelessness. If a man has a job, he can buy a house. If he hasn't got a job, even if you give him a house, he can't maintain it. So let's attack the real underlying problem. You'll only create a nation of owners if you create a nation of foxes. One of the questions I'm constantly asked is whether hedgehogs ever turn into foxes. The answer is yes – sometimes through sheer necessity caused by retrenchment from a large organisation. When push comes to shove, anyone can become a fox with a little bit of training. Foxes come in all shapes and sizes: the only proviso is that when beginners are asked to do the foxtrot, the band (in this case the government) provides the right beat. Another question I'm asked is whether hedgehog parents can have foxy children. Again, the reply is affirmative. Entrepreneurial offspring are a sign of youthful rebellion against staid parents! They know that it's better to be a fox off the leash than a fettered hedgehog.

Another recommendation to come out of the South African poverty summit I alluded to earlier is that the churches and other religious communities should become information centres for disadvantaged people. After all, it is part of the mission statement of these religious institutions to help the poor escape poverty. They not only have more outlets than Pick 'n Pay, they're open seven days a week too. They have virtually no turnover in the top echelons of their management structure; and they have competent frontline staff ministering to the spiritual needs of the public. Furthermore, these ministers spend sufficient time in a parish (six to eight years on average) to get to know the movers and shakers who can make things happen in the community.

From the proposed information centres, poor people could find out where to acquire skills; and where to write a business plan and get the start-up capital. Maybe, all the churches should be linked by computer so that the ministers can download the relevant information to their flock. People go to church on Sundays to confess their sins. After they have done so, they should be able to find out how to make some money! The Apostolic Faith Mission of South Africa is one church I know of that is training its ministers to offer more than prayers to retrenched members of the congregation. Twelve of its ministers (an aptly chosen number) are in the first group to be trained.

Another initiative is the Sakhisizwe Trust which has Beyers Naudé and Albertina Sisulu as joint patrons. It encompasses ten million people from different religious organisations. Sakhisizwe has formed Zimunathi Investments with the express intention of generating income to fund projects which will assist rural and urban foxes. Enlisted in the scheme already is the Informal Business Training Trust which is famous for its One-Up course culminating in a "Township MBA" being awarded to successful candidates. The Start-Up Fund, an ingenious microlending scheme where the incentive to repay is the promise of bigger loans, is also involved. Basically, this initiative brings together a trio of social foxes of long standing – André van Heerden, Cedric Buffler and Tony Davenport. They are all high-minded enough to see what needs to be done and hard-headed enough to make it happen. Good luck to them!

Ignorance was generally identified by the summit as the greatest impediment blocking poor people from progressing out of poverty. Another idea to overcome this problem was to launch a Poverty FM radio station to which listeners could tune in order to discover how other people were managing to escape the shackles of an existence on the breadline. Radio is the most powerful medium amongst poor people. Yet another idea was that the press should allocate so many column inches per week to stories on poverty-beaters – individuals who had through dint of hard work and application transformed themselves into self-sufficient foxes.

One fox made the following comment about the printed media the other day: "It is written by hedgehogs about hedgehogs, but that is probably because the bulk of the readership are hedgehogs too. Seldom, if ever, is there a positive article on township business. The world of foxes is all but invisible to journalists." I have more than a passing sympathy for the sentiment expressed by this fox. Go back to many early newspapers in South Africa and their front page was a series of classified advertisements for small business et al. Even *The Times* of London until fairly recently had that kind of format. In other words, newspapers used to be vehicles for foxes to get in touch with one another and make the public aware of their existence. Nowadays, the lead stories and editorials are confined to the comings and goings of this or that political hedgehog. Even British newspapers are better than South African ones at carrying interesting stories of ordinary individuals with everyday foibles and the things they get up to. It's a pity the foxes are neglected here; if they do merit a mention, the likely reason is that they've done something wrong or some calamity has befallen them. The news is seldom good.

Having got that off my chest, I have to say that there is one newspaper in South Africa which caters absolutely for foxes. It's called *Big News for Small Business*. It is published in Cape Town and is now two years old. Every month, 25 000 free copies are distributed to small entrepreneurs, ranging from shop owners to building contractors and manufacturers on the Cape Flats. It has just gone national with a potential audience of 200 000 entrepreneurs. The best page of the paper is the "Directory of small business support". It lists all the places where you can get finance, training and counselling, advice on tendering, information about flea markets, etc. Every other page is peppered with photographs of beaming foxes who are on their way to their first million rand!

A brilliant example of a poverty-beating community is Stutterheim in the Eastern Cape. It has managed to change its destiny from a town crippled by violence, poverty and racial tension to one in which its residents have together woven an amazing tapestry of self-reliant, industrious enterprises. There's more money now in Stutterheim; but, more important still, the velocity of that money is rising in line with the increasing number of transactions between residents. Like a chain reaction in nuclear physics, the economic growth in Stutterheim is self-sustaining. The two foxes leading this transformation are Chris Magwangqana and Nico Ferreira. In fact, the Stutterheim story has become such a legend in the land that many other towns desperately want to copy them. But they're going to have to find champion foxes similar to Chris and Nico to lead their packs. In fact, the best answer is a school for social foxes where community development officers can be trained and the Stutterheim experience can be shared. A school on these lines opened its doors in Bethnal Green in London in 1998. The leading light behind the project is Michael Young (who was previously responsible for the establishment of the Open University). It is called the School for Social Entrepreneurs.

In Zimbabwe, I came across a spot which must have the greatest concentration of foxes per hectare of land in southern Africa. It's called Siya So, which in Shona means "Leave it so". Siya So is part of Mbare, one of the oldest suburbs in Harare. It presents two starkly contrasting pictures. On the one hand, you see extreme destitution, grime, poverty and people working with dangerous chemicals and exposed electricity wires. The roads aren't tarred and the factories are ramshackle affairs without proper roofs. It must turn into an impassable quagmire after heavy rains. Yet, on the other hand, you see the triumph of entrepreneurship over poverty with all kinds of workshops doing all kinds of things. These are people who see opportunities in the midst of desperation and desolation. They create something of tangible value from what most of us would have thrown away. Leather goods, home-made water pumps, battery and car repairs (one garage advertised that it specialised in "non-runners"), security fencing – in Siya So you can find anything. Up the road are coffin manufacturers who sadly can't keep up with the surge in demand caused by the AIDS epidemic. The most striking example of success was a manufacturer of lampshades, chairs and tables, many of which are exported to New York and Tokyo.

The centre of Harare itself is fast becoming a CFD (Central Fox District). I visited one office block which had been converted into a honeycomb of small businesses. The landlord's policy was not to rent out floors or rooms, but each desk inside a room for Z$250 a month. In one room, there were eleven desks all manned by people involved in the manufacture of clothing. This was a sweat shop with a difference. Each desk was an independent business and the room as a whole a voluntary co-operative of eleven foxes. When I asked one of them why she didn't make dresses at home rent-free, she replied: "Because I can make twice as many dresses a month in this room. Over there is the person who cuts the cloth, in that corner is an overlocker and I've got my ordinary sewing machine here. We get many more bulk orders as a team than if each of us worked individually at home." Although the whole set-up might have been condemned by any one of the more vocal international human rights organisations, in its way it was a fabulous example of foxes beating poverty. Perhaps all those empty office blocks in downtown Johannesburg will be put to the same use. Like education, architecture has to be adapted to the new concept of work.

Generally, in regard to poverty alleviation, one burning question often repeats itself: why do hedgehogs always propose a "National Plan of Action" which gets you from A to Z in one fell swoop? Apart from the phrase in itself being an oxymoron, it engenders a feeling of despair that we will ever get to grips with the problem, given its enormity. Foxes plant acorns, see which ones grow fastest and then replicate those varieties elsewhere. "We shall overcome," say foxes, "but bit by bit, softly, softly."

Profile of a fox

People often question me about the characteristics of a modern-day fox. Apart from being bright-eyed and bushy-tailed, foxes are first and foremost focused. Once they've selected their target niche in the market, they let nothing distract them. They concentrate their energy and pounce on an opportunity before anyone else has discovered it. They turn their ideas into action very fast. And what's more they don't let go. Focused foxes remain cool, whatever the weather.

One of the reasons foxes can retain composure is the emphasis they give to vertical communication from the top to the bottom of the organisation they are running. They get everybody on their side. They realise the devil is in the detail when it comes to implementation. MBWA – management by walking around – is therefore their style. Hedgehogs, on the other hand, indulge in horizontal communication with one another at power breakfasts and never get beyond the generalities of the topic under discussion. Their span of responsibility is usually too wide for them to give enough energy to any single issue. In a funny way, this fact is responsible for the collapse of not only centrally planned economies but also some corporate giants. The organisation simply becomes too big for even the most intelligent mind to absorb the myriad of details necessary to make a rational decision.

These days we talk of exploiting windows of opportunity because the market frequently consists of short-term bubbles of value that come and go. We're in a world of shifting sands. If you're first in there, you make the most profit. If you snooze, you lose. Foxes understand that if there is a treasure trove to be had from a particular niche, millions of other foxes will soon be around to drive the margins down. For example, Bill Gates is very much aware that his Windows programme is now under threat from "open-source" software systems like Linux and Java. What will he do next? However, foxes are smart and never put all their eggs into the first basket that comes their way. They don't want to be wiped out on the initial occasion. In the field of mutual fund management, these principles are being applied all the time except that it's about picking stocks that are undervalued and riding with them until everybody knows and the shares are fully priced. Then you move on.

A glorious example of spotting and exploiting a bubble of value happened in South Africa a few years back. A young lady just out of university started in the conference business. She decided to go for broke with her first event and invited one of the top international business gurus to host a day's workshop in Johannesburg and Cape Town. She rang him up in November and asked him whether he was available. He responded that, unfortunately, he was totally booked up for the following year. She twisted his arm by saying that this was Madiba-land and couldn't he come before his official itinerary in the new year kicked off. He was obviously taken with her persistence because he said okay, he would pencil in two days in early January. "However," he went on, "I am the highest paid speaker on the circuit and charge $100 000 a day." Undaunted, our South African fox told him to pencil in the visit and she would ring back and confirm in December. She then desktop-published a flyer advertising the event with a price tag of R4 000 per individual attending – justified on the grounds that the guru had never been here before. She received a large quantity of affirmative answers in Johannesburg and a smaller number in Cape Town. And because she requested a cheque with each confirmation slip, she managed to bank a couple of million rand up front. Accordingly, she contacted the guru and told him to come. The two conferences took place as scheduled and the guru suitably impressed his audience. She paid him his fee of R700 000 (at the time one dollar was equivalent to R3,50). The remainder of her expenses on hotels, travel, etc. amounted to several hundred thousand rand. The net result was a handsome profit made out of thin air and without taking any risk at all. Now that's what I call foxy!

Another superb example was a young photographer who set up shop in the grounds of the Union Buildings in Pretoria. It was the occasion of some large demonstration. He had a cardboard cut-out of Nelson Mandela and, for a suitable fee, he offered demonstrators the chance of being photographed with the State President in front of the pillars of government. A nice little bubble of value for him. So is the Y2K bug for foxy programmers. They charge considerable amounts by the hour for rewriting codes, so that planes don't fall out of the sky or bank balances disappear when the clock strikes midnight on 31 December 1999.

One of the principal reasons for focus is competition, whether you are large or small. It is so intense these days that you cannot take your eye off the ball. Speaking of which, it is now inconceivable that anybody would represent his or her country at more than one major sport. Fifty years ago, Denis Compton played cricket and soccer for England. And those were the days when England could play both cricket and soccer. Today, people would fall off their chairs if Hansie Cronjé took off his cricket gloves and put on soccer boots to play for Bafana Bafana, the South African football team. Focus is a special quality demanded of chess players. When Bobby Fischer beat Boris Spassky for the title of World Champion in 1972, in Reykjavik, Iceland, it was apparent to anyone watching the match that Fischer's concentration burned up his opponent. He must have been foxy to have become the youngest grandmaster in history at the age of 15.

However, focus (and passion for that matter) should not be confused with obsession. It is very easy to become so focused that you develop myopia in your outlook. Then you start acting like a hedgehog, i.e. you arrogantly assume that there is nothing else to life besides your business occupation and your own self-interest. Then you run the risk of sacrificing family, friends, hobbies and even your basic morality on the altar of winning the race. As I said earlier on, foxes are driven by the credo that life does not revolve around one big thing but getting the balance right between many little things. So be focused but don't cross the fine line into selfishness and obsession. You'll be the poorer for doing so. Remember the ancient Greek saying, that in the wake of hubris comes nemesis. Never take yourself too seriously. Those that do always end up making serious mistakes.

The other day, I was at a lunch at a house overlooking Pringle Bay near Cape Town. I had a fascinating conversation with a film director, Martine de la Harpe. She quickly proved herself a fellow travelling fox by explaining that the first thing she was taught at film school in New York was what not to do. Most first-time directors try to visualise the whole film at the outset and dream that if it can be put together in one perfect reel, it will take the world by storm. Actually, making a film is as much about process as product, namely building it up one scene at a time and seeing where it goes. Each little bit of dialogue, each action shot can change the way you approach the next scene – and you'll never know beforehand how each section will pan out. So while you obviously must have an overall scenario to guide you, you must not be too straitjacketed by the script. Focus has to be tempered by a series of spontaneous judgements of how the next shot can best be taken. This observation rang bells with me. For instance, the presentation which led to this book was built up that way – a broad concept combined with flashes of inspiration from all the sources I tapped as I went along.

She then elaborated on the "bagel" theory propounded by one of her friends. A bagel is a hard bread roll in the shape of a ring. Basically, we have been deluged with so much propaganda about the "vision thing" and aspiring to ever greater heights of achievement that we pass clean through the centre of the bagel without ever tasting it. We are so concerned about what is around the corner, over the next rise, etc. that we fail to appreciate the here and now – the 24-hour period that we are currently in. We do not stop to smell the roses when the only real thing about life could be the roses! Hedgehogs who spend week after week scurrying from one meeting to another in a constant state of anticipation end up with a stream of pseudo-experiences. Contrary to this, foxes who grow their own herbs, cook their own meals, pack their lives with little things and savour each moment in itself and for itself are the richer for such an existence. You may say that veering off to taste the bagel completely opposes the notion of focus. Foxes, though, understand the oriental philosophy of the "yin" and the "yang". For every quality in life, there's a contrary one to consider at the same time. As Isaiah Berlin stated, nothing is absolutely valid (except certain laws of mathematics and ethics).

One of the highlights of my stay in Anglo's Gold Division had nothing to do with gold. We had a magic relay team that won the Investec and First National Bank company relays. Part of the prize for our eight runners was to compete in the Chicago relay, which they won, and then in the ultimate relay-of-all-relays in New York where all the winners of these races from around the USA participated. They won that too! For the small amount of encouragement I gave them, it was a big bite out of the bagel.

Bill Gates was a focused fox when he was young. His interest in computer software was first stimulated when he reprogrammed his school computer to play tick-tack-toe (what we call noughts and crosses). Later on, he designed a programme to control traffic in Seattle. Then he made the big discovery that you could programme microprocessors like mainframes. Thus Microsoft was born and the rest, as they say, is history. His personal fortune is legendary. Suppose you spent R100 every second from the moment you were born to the moment you died, you wouldn't get through it – even if you lived to be a hundred. However, the sheer size of his fortune has brought its own problems. He is increasingly being viewed as a mighty hedgehog rather than a nifty fox. The same fate was experienced by John D

Rockefeller, the son of a snake-oil salesman, who built up Standard Oil. Undoubtedly a fox when he shook down the oil industry in the late 19th century, he eventually achieved a net worth equivalent to two percent of America's GDP in 1913. Such a share in current terms would be worth $190 billion, or more than three times as much as Gates is worth. It's a salutary lesson for all foxes: the more successful you get, the harder it is to be perceived as a fox.

The second attribute of a fox is differentiation. Foxes realise that, in an era of constant surpluses, selling the same product to the same public as everybody else doesn't make you money. More of the same gets you nowhere. The only sustainable way of preserving a healthy profit margin is to be different or unique in some way. Hedgehogs have come to a similar conclusion but regard size as the sole criterion of difference. They embark on a combination of mergers and acquisition to become the dominant force in their field and achieve the greatest economies of scale. Biggest is best to hedgehogs. They chase each other down the unit cost curve in a game of "anything you can do, I can do better". But occasionally a Goliath comes unstuck. A David emerges from the wings and, with a single slingshot, slays the big guy with something new and special.

The foxes in the spaza shops in the township trade at the other end of the spectrum to the hedgehogs. They take bags of sugar and mealie meal and divide them up into small sachets which contain minor quantities which are not available at other stores. They offer the customer the convenience of buying in small lots. It is their specialisation. Hence, they can add a significant mark-up on the price at which they purchase the commodity in bulk from the hedgehogs.

The top foxes don't just want to be better or cheaper than the competition; they want to make it irrelevant. To this end, Dell Computer pioneered the direct selling of personal computers to your home. No need to go to a shop anymore, and now everyone is scrambling to copy Dell. Dr John Pemberton was a fox in 1886 when he invented the formula for Coca-Cola syrup. It is still going strong because there is nothing like it. Buddy Holly was a fox because nobody else had a singing voice like him. Although he was only 22 when he died in a light-aircraft crash in February 1959, his impact on the world of music has been truly phenomenal. But you don't have to invent exotic products or write a song like "Peggy Sue" to be a top fox. Equally, your field of endeavour doesn't have to be hot and hi-tech like the Internet. You can take an ordinary business and do something special with it. Take McDonald's. They're foxes because they have perfected the concept of fast food in clean and friendly surroundings. Prompt service with a world-class smile is what differentiates them. Take Nando's in South Africa. Robert Brozin, the founder, is a fox because he realised that chicken tastes extra special when covered in a Portuguese sauce! Often nothing more is needed than the warmth of a receptionist's voice when he or she greets a potential customer for the first time.

An example of a fox I came across in Namibia is the owner of a restaurant at Langstrand, halfway between Walvis Bay and Swakopmund. He offers dinners in the desert to the passengers of cruise ships that dock at Walvis Bay. For two hundred Europeans, there's no experience in Europe which equals a crayfish braai among the dunes and under the stars. It's unique. In contrast, anybody selling those animal sculptures in the centre of Harare or Windhoek or outside the Rosebank Mall in Johannesburg is definitely not a fox. The market is saturated, implying that margins must be razor-thin if not nonexistent.

To become foxes on the subcontinent of Africa, we must start developing coherent African brands. Increasingly, consumers are buying the experience that goes with the product rather than the product itself, because it's hard to distinguish physically between products nowadays. Take American jeans. We buy them because the very act of putting them on makes us think of prairies, rodeos and cowboys. Or we just want to get closer to Brooke Shields or Brad Pitt. A Harley-Davidson motorcycle is a reminder of the classic movie *Easy Rider* with Peter Fonda and Jack Nicholson. It's a nice way for middle-aged men to rediscover their adolescent fantasies. American products sell because Americans believe in America. Most Americans are not in possession of passports because they never travel outside America. Why leave the best place on Earth?

Well, we've got to start believing in Africa just as strongly if we want to sell African products to Americans. And the potential is there. The very word "Africa" conjures up far more exciting and sensuous images in the minds of Americans than say the word "Australia". Australia may be Crocodile Dundee country, but we're seen as more different – we possess a greater "buzz". Apart from tourism, which is an obvious area to develop strong African brands, other industries might include clothing, jewellery, furniture, etc. The point about foxes is that they have the confidence to be different instead of imitating others. If we want to be African foxes, we must positively exploit our national and cultural roots. We must drop the dreadful paradigm that imported products are always better than locally produced ones. This lack of belief in ourselves is directly responsible for our urge to conform and imitate. But Americans don't want pseudo-American products from Africa. They want the real African thing.

What sets America apart from the rest of the world is that immigrants feel such a sense of ownership about the place that before too long they say they're American. Whether they're Italians, Irish, Chinese, Mexican, Brazilian or even British, they eventually downplay – or even forget – their country of origin. The acid test for us, therefore, will be when we have American immigrants coming here and saying – after they've absorbed our culture – that they're Africans. Right now, that may sound far-fetched, but it has to be the goal.

Let me give you four specific examples to illustrate the potential and actual power of African branding. And these represent only the tip of the hippo's ears (better than iceberg as a catch phrase, don't you think?). I was in Bond Street in London the other day and saw a gold chain on display in the window of a jeweller. I went in and asked to see the piece. The salesman dutifully brought it to me, whereupon I pulled a spring balance out of my pocket and weighed it. He was shocked and said that nobody had ever weighed a piece in the shop since it was established in 1751. I asked him: "How do you know?" Anyway, it transpired from a hasty calculation that the contained gold in the piece was being sold for $2 700 an ounce. So, with clever design and branding, you can multiply the value of bullion by a factor of nine. Shouldn't we therefore be producing gold jewellery which has a unique, ethnic design and is sold under the banner "real gold from Africa"? Italy makes more money out of gold than South Africa and yet Italy doesn't mine any. Tells you something, doesn't it!

Furthermore, while we're on the subject of Italy, the Italian Renaissance had nothing to do with politics. It wasn't announced in advance as something to be striven for. The phrase applied in retrospect to the sum total of the works by many different artistic foxes expressing their brilliant talent as individuals. Moreover, it wasn't the government that bankrolled the artists. Rich banking families such as the Medicis became their patrons. We will only be able to talk about an African Renaissance when African art, African music and African designs are taking the world by storm; big business sees it as a genuine investment opportunity; and African foxes are the toast of the town!

In this regard, the second example comes from the Mzilikazi art and craft centre in Bulawayo. The sculptors there are world class. I spotted a set of clay figurines portraying people in earnest conversation about a problem one of them had. The concern on their faces and the gestures they were making made it one of the most animated scenes I'd ever seen in that art form. I asked the person responsible for this magnificent work how much he wanted for it. He answered Z$1 000. Compared to current prices in this medium in the international art market, I reckoned he had seriously underpriced himself. That set would have easily fetched £1 000 in London.

The third example I love to quote is of some travel agents in Cape Town who are marketing the Karoo as a unique African experience to German tourists. "Come and sleep under African skies without fear of being mugged" goes their slogan. In response, thousands of Germans are flying to Cape Town and, instead of going down the Garden Route to Port Elizabeth, they are dispersing through the Karoo to places like Beaufort West, Graaff-Reinet and even De Aar. And the fastest growing business in the Karoo has nothing to do with agriculture. It is the bed-and-breakfast industry offering world-class, personalised service to German tourists.

The fourth example relates to a man who draws packed audiences whenever he goes to London from South Africa. He tells the story of the Battle of Isandlwana at which the Zulus demolished a regiment of the British Army when Britain was at the height of its military power in 1879. He follows this with an account of what happened at Rorke's

Drift, during the evening of the same day, when a heavily outnumbered British contingent of 110 men held off their Zulu attackers and in the process won more Victoria Crosses than in any other engagement before or since. His name is David Rattray, and it is precisely because he tells the story from both the British and Zulu perspectives that he is so popular. He is different in that he has totally absorbed Zulu culture. He is a Zulu fox (like Johnny Clegg who has consistently topped the French music charts and was nicknamed "Le Zulu Blanc").

The third quality of foxes is to think beyond their immediate terrain. An Israeli fox whom I met in Jerusalem a couple of years ago was wearing a T-shirt which said: "Don't worry America, Israel is behind you." It's that kind of "can-do" attitude that makes you a fox. We still suffer from an inferiority complex here. What on earth could Benoni produce, we ask, that is world class? The answer is Charlize Theron! Never in the history of business has it been easier to take a niched product and market it worldwide. For instance, there's a German company that makes an aquarium for one type of tropical fish which needs a very special flow of water and a particular temperature. If either are slightly out of kilter, the fish dies. But there are enough lovers of this sensitive little fish around the world to make it a highly profitable enterprise. It bears out the mantra "be focused, be unique, go global".

Right now, a fox would regard the depreciation of our local currencies as a golden opportunity to penetrate foreign markets or to attract tourists to come here. He or she could literally take a leaf out of the book of Jeff Bezos. He's an American who set up a web site on the Internet and invited people from anywhere in the world to hit his site and demand any book title. He guaranteed that he would deliver the book within a few days and at a cheaper price than most bookshops. Now his company, *amazon.com*, has two and half million titles on offer. It is worth hundreds of millions of dollars and he is giving bookshops everywhere a run for their money. CDnow is doing precisely the same in the music retail business. As an online retailer, it has 350 000 titles to choose from (compared to 100 000 in Tower Records in Tokyo, the largest music store in the world).

Perhaps we should be developing a series of web sites offering unique products and services to the rest of the world. In fact, *buy-Afrika.com* has done just that. It is performing the role of intermediary between the overseas market and talented South African manufacturers of everything from curtains with intricate Xhosa designs to beaded decorations for Christmas trees. So, stick some graphics of your product on the Internet and see what happens. You might get a thousand hits. Nevertheless, a lesson which our foxes are going to have to learn is how to scale up production when a large order is received. I heard of one Transkei potter who was told that a large retail chain in America wanted 10 000 exact copies of a cup he'd made. He scratched his head in amazement and said: "You're kidding. How can I repeat a work of art so many times?!"

Another area of great potential on the Internet is tourism. Already you can call up pictures of the hotels and other accommodation at a particular location; then a menu of the ways of getting there; then the prices of the different alternatives of accommodation and travel. Then click, you can book and pay. The mouse does everything. It's a heaven-sent opportunity for South Africa with its unique diversity of fauna and flora to enter every household and travel agent's office around the world with access to the Internet. Clifton Beach in Cape Town has already gone live on the Internet. A camera scanning the beach takes a photograph every 10 seconds and transmits it to the web site. By 2002, global online retail sales relating to travel on the Internet are expected to lie between $12 billion and $26 billion per annum. Despite the title of this book, I have to make one observation about the millennium: the Internet to the next one will be what Gutenberg's printing press was to this one – the most influential innovation of all. It will genuinely turn the world into a "global village".

Like focus, however, globalisation has its drawbacks. It can play havoc with family life. Executives constantly in mid-air from one continent to another find it hard to "be there" for the important occasions of their children. Their friends never know whether they're "at home" in the houses they have dotted around the world. Consequently, they never get asked out except to functions relating to their business. However geographically dispersed our possessions are, we all suffer from one limitation: we only have one body which can be in one place at one time. Foxes who successfully find a global niche must watch out that they don't turn into hollow hedgehogs who in a futile way try to ignore this limitation.

The fourth attribute of a fox is to have a perpetual spirit of innovation. Never stop and be complacent, because the competition will catch up. Like riding a bicycle, you have to keep moving along or fall off. Think of the Japanese. They were at the height of their power of innovation in the 1970s. The VCR, the video camera, the Walkman, the just-in-time stores management system, the zero-defect manufacturing process – wow! new products and ideas poured out of Japan in those days. But in the 1980s they started believing in their own public relations and all the flattery that was being heaped on them. They relaxed and took their foot off the innovation pedal. Meanwhile, the Americans put their foot down hard because they were being assaulted from all sides by Japanese goods. And, voilà, they have come up with the innovation of the 1990s – Viagra – whereas the Japanese economy has gone into a tailspin.

Innovation comes in small steps with an occasional great leap forward. But you have to have that frame of mind which considers ideas no matter how wild or ridiculous. Take the producer in Hollywood who thought you could make another blockbuster movie about a liner that sinks. James Cameron was right! He used the same formula as *Gone with the Wind* – a love affair against the backdrop of a national tragedy – and got the same awesome results at the box office. Andy Grove is the foxy Chairman of Intel, which makes the Pentium chip. He wrote a book a few years ago called *Only the Paranoid Survive*. The title may be slightly over the top but it correctly surmises that complacency is the enemy of success. Intel spends billions of dollars on research and development to stay ahead in the chip game. David Packard was also a fox when he ran Hewlett Packard. He made sure that everybody from the factory floor upwards contributed to the innovation process through the formation of "skunk works" – small teams which examined every aspect of the business. He knew that shop-floor knowledge counts, so product and organisational improvement couldn't only be left to the pointy-headed scientists and management consultants. Now 70 per cent of Hewlett Packard's annual revenue is made up of products invented in the previous two years. In other words, it's as important to be the midwife for other people's original ideas as to be the innovator yourself.

Fifthly, foxes are flexible. They know when to switch direction, because they have a sixth sense for danger. They are open-minded to the fact that the market suddenly moves off in a completely new direction which can mean that their product is going out of fashion and their business is becoming a nonbusiness. Foxes embrace uncertainty and turbulence which they see as throwing up new opportunities. They only plan as far ahead as they understand. They change what they can and adapt to what they can't. As important, they don't change what they shouldn't. They are experts at weighing up risk versus reward when allocating capital. They accept that all the computer runs in the world do not replace a good "nose" or instinct for business. They realise that, even with a brilliant idea, timing is everything. For all these reasons, many managers make lousy entrepreneurs when they are elevated to a level where they're making the strategic decisions. Having been hedgehogs all their lives, they are thrust into the role of foxes with no preparation and little inclination to change.

Foxy companies understand that focus should not be equated with rigidity. They engage in sequential focus whereby each step in a new direction demands a new focus. Take 3M, which used to be called Minnesota Mining and Manufacturing. It first focused on mining, then sandpaper, then scotch tape, then post-it notes, and now hi-tech optical products. Over time it metamorphosed itself in line with market conditions, but never lost its main strength – being a leader in serial innovation. A foxy organisation has no idea what it's going to be like in 25 years' time. As one 3M executive said: "You have to kiss a lot of frogs to find the prince. But, remember, one prince can pay for a lot of frogs."

A foxy matrix to draw up is one that assesses the vulnerability of the various parts of your business to change. It has core/noncore on one axis and dog/star on the other. We all know what to do with core stars – keep them. Equally, we all know what to do with noncore dogs – get rid of them. Where doubt creeps in is with core dogs and noncore stars. Can you turn around the one and redefine your business to retain the other? Is a noncore star about to become a noncore dog so that it should be disposed of now? This is where an open and detached mind is a prerequisite for smart decision-making. Perhaps, in the state of perpetual transition which our markets are in at the moment, the only sensible approach is to go the 3M route and change the definition of "core" as we go along.

There's a foxy farmer in Bloemfontein who has decided that growing maize and keeping cattle has become a non-business in light of falling prices. So he has turned his farm into a rose garden. He grows roses and flies them out to Antwerp and Amsterdam. Other farmers thought he was mad but now he is one of the most profitable farmers in the Free State. At another farm, the owner discovered that the reeds which grew in his vlei made perfect saxophone reeds. After many years of just looking at them and admiring their symmetrical shape, he re-perceived their value. He decided to take a sample to the largest manufacturer of reeds for musical instruments in the world, based in France. They were knocked out by the quality of the sample and immediately placed a substantial order. The reeds are now a major source of the farmer's income. Foxes turn anything into an asset through lateral thinking. Around Nylstroom in the Northern Province, foxy farmers are moving out of farming altogether by combining their properties into malaria-free, big-five game parks. In direct contrast, the farmers that go on hoeing the same row that their fathers and grandfathers did are the ones who lose out and ask for drought relief. You need a radar system permanently switched on to conduct 360-degree sweeps of the market. It's the bombshell you don't expect that does you in. Yet, it's often serendipity that lifts you up. As Gary Player, one of the golfing greats, once said: "The more I practise, the luckier I get."

The sixth quality of foxes is to gather other shrewd foxes around them. Foxes seldom run businesses singly, because they know they may not get the money from the bank or the stock exchange if they approach either of them solo. They also know that they will never achieve the same degree of creative energy by themselves as that which they can get by participating in small teams, where individuals spark off each other.

This is also why foxes cluster their businesses. Visit any small town in northern Italy and you'll see astonishing results. Castel Goffredo has 7 000 people but produces nearly half of Europe's hosiery. In Udine, 800 furniture manufacturers produce half of Europe's chairs. Meanwhile, Sassuolo's 180 ceramic factories account for two-thirds of all imported tiles around the world. The average workforce of Italy's 450 machine-tool makers is only 70 employees. But again, because of clustering, they are a potent force and put Italy behind Japan, Germany and America as the fourth-largest machine-tool manufacturer in the world.

Visit any informal trading area in southern Africa and you will find clothes, say, in one section, food in another, pots and pans in a third, etc. Foxes give and take from one another. They co-operate and compete with one another at the same time. More importantly, a cluster is a way of attaining critical mass for attracting customers, which an individual business may not be able to do. Mutare, which lies close to the Mozambican border in Zimbabwe, has one of the largest flea markets in southern Africa, specialising in clothes. People come from miles around because of the bargains available there. Brand-new dresses and suits are available for R20, and brand-new blouses for 50 cents. Apparently, many of these items were donated by British charities to Mozambicans who prefer food to clothes and therefore smuggle the latter across the border for resale. I wonder what Oxfam would have to say about that. Foxes will always tweak a system to their advantage.

Another method of clustering used by foxes is the formation of co-operatives which bring economies of scale to a particular stage in the production and marketing chain. Farmers have for a long time pooled their resources to have common storage and distribution facilities, but now the concept has taken a new turn in America with "roll-ups". A roll-up incorporates dozens of small businesses into a single, loosely controlled corporate entity which gives maximum autonomy on the ground to each small business but gives them collectively the benefits of centralised purchasing, payroll administration and other support services. Foxes owning travel agencies and funeral parlours have particularly taken advantage of this kind of structure. Roll-ups are now quoted on Nasdaq and have attracted considerable investor interest. Here, the Johannesburg General Hospital is an ideal candidate for becoming a roll-up. I doubt whether it can ever be managed again as a single, monolithic entity.

Foxes also grant their colleagues a stake in the business with shares or share options so that everybody's interests are aligned. Foxy farmers in South Africa are offering their workers shares in their farms. They know that some form of collective ownership of the farm by the people who work there is a better defence against confiscation than sole ownership by a single individual. Foxy American companies also make performance-related pay half the overall remuneration package of their talented employees. Think about that one. The average bonus of a high-performance American fox is 100 per cent over and above his or her basic pay. That's remarkably different to the human resources policy adopted by some South African companies which enshrines the principle of equal misery for all. It's hedgehog stuff that everybody should get the same amount, regardless of contribution. Foxy companies don't mind significant pay-outs to individuals who have enhanced the bottom line because the company still gets to keep the lion's share of the incremental profit generated by their efforts.

On another score, foxes definitely go for establishing family businesses where they can, because they know that family members can be trusted. Taiwan has survived the Asian collapse better than any other country in the Far East solely on account of its economy being a network of family businesses. In fact, most foxes raising capital for the first time scrounge money from their families and friends. The more foxes, therefore, involved at the inception of a business, the more families and friends that can be approached as potential investors!

Obtaining a franchise is also a strategy considered by a fox. Having the brand name and backing of a big business but, on the other hand, being the owner of your own franchise frequently offers the best balance for a fox. I'm surprised that there are not more franchised operations in South Africa and it is something that should be pursued.

The seventh quality of a fox is to be decent to your customers, to your employees and to nature and the environment. It is unfair to think of a fox as a sly creature which causes mayhem in the coop. Foxes realise that it is in their long-term interest not to rip people off. Be smart but be fair. Make a profit but offer value for money. Be lean and cost-effective, but pay your employees well. One foxy English company measures the happiness of its workforce as part of an annual social audit and publishes the result. Imagine that – indexing happiness as well as productivity. Foxes are good animals! They attract young people with upright values to join them. In fact, one foxy merchant bank in New York makes its young stars go and do two days of meals-on-wheels a month in Harlem. The latter see the other side of the tracks that way.

A foxy farmer in Upington, the hottest area in South Africa, grows sultana grapes and exports them all to a major retail chain in the United Kingdom. On four occasions, this chain has sent out a team to audit his quality control, the pesticides he uses, the accommodation of his employees, their conditions of service, his environmental, health and safety policy, his performance against this policy, etc. If he doesn't pass the audit, he loses the contract. For this reason, I believe the remuneration of managers in any company should be based on a variety of factors which are given equal weighting including safety record, environmental conduct, integrity as well as production and financial performance.

John Elkington is a foxy British environmentalist who has created a lot of waves worldwide with his concept of the "triple bottom line". In a nutshell, companies should pursue a combination of economic, social and environmental goals and find a sensible midpoint inside the triangle. This is absolutely in line with the philosophy of a fox I outlined earlier that life is about getting the little things right even if they conflict with one another. Green hedgehogs and business hedgehogs are as bad as each other. The former press the environmental button so hard that, if they are to be believed, we should all go back to eating berries and riding bicycles. The latter press the profit button so hard that any economic boom will assuredly be followed by an environmental bust. I prefer foxes from both sides who seek common ground.

In Toronto, Canada, a nice illustration of the triple bottom line presented itself recently. It all started with the discovery that small birds fly into lit skyscrapers at night. For several years, a band of volunteers have been scouring the pavements early in the morning to rescue those birds which are still alive. They are also pressurising building owners and occupants to switch off the office lights when they leave, and are regularly photographing progress. It's a triple benefit: birds, energy and money are all being saved.

Hence, to be good at business, you have to be good in business. Social foxes who run the NGOs get their kicks out of being givers, not takers. That's quite a shrewd mission in life because you only remember people who've given of themselves to you and blatantly gone against their own self-interest on the odd occasion. Takers are instantly forgettable. I attended the memorial service the other day of a fox I knew. Like me, he was one of South Africa's great optimists. In a beautiful tribute, his son chose to draw our attention to the minor acts of kindness that his father was capable of – such as purchasing an entire catch of fish on one occasion and a whole tray of peaches on another when the sellers obviously couldn't find other buyers. He was a fox for all seasons. As I said earlier on, the little things in life are the ones that count in the end. It's not the stuff you put in your curriculum vitae that captures people's imagination after you're gone.

Social foxes are mavericks who go against the flow in the name of what they think is right. Gavin Relly, to whom this book is dedicated, was a consummate businessman. But he will be remembered as much for being the leader of a group of private sector representatives who went to Lusaka, in September 1985, for a ground-breaking meeting with the ANC. He was also a generous boss in allowing me to do the scenario roadshow in 1986 and to disseminate the conclusions of Anglo's scenario team to the public. A lesser man would have vetoed the idea of publishing the research on the grounds that it was an internal study to help Anglo, not outsiders. Jim Jones, editor of *Business Day*, opened his tribute to Gavin with the words: "If there is one characteristic for which Gavin Relly will be remembered, it was his fundamental decency. All else about him, including his accomplishments, sprang from that." Like the true fox that he was, he made business fun for himself and those around him. He made everybody feel like a somebody. It was always a pleasure going into his office. And he'd always find something humorous to say to lighten a discussion. He once told me: "Sometimes you have to avoid giving advice and let a person hit the wall. It's the only way he'll learn." Obviously, Gavin occasionally gave the thumbs up to the Vesuvius model!

The eighth and last attribute is passion. Successful foxes are passionate about their work and life generally. Recently, in Grahamstown, I came across a sprightly, retired general practitioner called Dr Mary Knowling who personified this characteristic. Her passion is to rehabilitate the interior of the cathedral there which has the tallest spire in the country. She and several assistants have restored the choir stalls, scrubbed the mosaic in the floor, had the stained-glass windows expertly repaired, and cleaned the interior sandstone walls. No mean feat for someone over seventy years old. It's never too late to be a fox because age does not dull this animal. Plenty of entrepreneurs start businesses in their sixties after they've retired from conventional careers. A splendid example is Ely Callaway. He used his knowledge of aeronautics to design the Great Big Bertha, a golf club which has spectacularly lengthened the drives of amateur golfers around the world.

Albert Mathibe is also a fox. He lives in "the ruralest of the rural, the dustiest of the dusty, the poorest of the poor" villages in the Northern Province – Patantswana. There's no signpost to this place. It just says "to the mountains". His passion has been the establishment of a community centre with a library, clinic and preschool/daycare facility in Patantswana. A local curse goes: "Anyone who does not dream must not sleep." He can sleep soundly!

The third fox I would like to mention is Rosemary Nalden. She is a freelance viola player from England who managed to persuade over a hundred classical musicians to do a simultaneous busk at 16 mainline railway stations across Britain. In two hours they raised enough money to enable her to buy stringed instruments for young people in Soweto. She teaches them herself in a tiny church office and has moulded them into a little gem of an orchestra. Her dream to build a proper music centre in the township will shortly come to fruition. She reckons that there's a greater concentration of music talent in Soweto than in Hampstead, the suburb of choice for the intelligentsia in London. Moreover, she believes that Soweto could become the heartbeat for classical music in Africa. SSQ – The Soweto String Quartet – offer a glimpse of things to come.

I deliberately chose three social foxes as illustrations because the passion to make a difference is just as important as the passion to make money. However, let me tell you of an old American fox, who is just a little less rich than Bill Gates. He was asked the other day to define passion. He said: "I have always wanted to play golf with Tiger Woods. Supposing I got the chance and I shot three under par on the first nine holes and I was one up on Tiger going into the clubhouse for tea. Then my cellphone rang and it was a broker telling me my company's stock had fallen 10 per cent. I'd immediately excuse myself and go straight to the office to find out what was wrong. You see, my company is my life." Looking at the CEOs of the most admired companies in America, they have widely different personalities. Some are outspoken, others shy and retiring. But they all share this one characteristic – passion.

The status of a fox

The most important thing we can do in the short term is to improve the status of the fox in South Africa. We exalt politicians, academics, lawyers and sports heroes, but the humble entrepreneur is considered to be someone who failed to make the cut in the formal sector. He or she must be a refugee, freelance hobo or poor cousin from the country to have to resort to owning a small business. The more extreme perception is that an entrepreneur is close to being a crook – a money-grabbing, greasy, fast-talking spiv who shouldn't be let in your front door. And heaven forbid that your son or your daughter should ever show signs of being a fox. Not in my home, you won't.

What nonsense! What a shame that we have inherited Europe's snobbish attitude to foxes when Europe has an unemployment rate triple that of America. If a fox strikes it rich in Europe, he is immediately branded as nouveau riche. In America new money is every bit as good as old money. Gates's wealth is as much revered as Rockefeller's. Somehow we must absorb the American mindset that foxes are the salt of the earth. Pioneering foxes made America. The little guy burrowing away in some garage in Silicon Valley who may one day knock Bill Gates off his perch with his invention is in his own way as extraordinary as Tiger Woods. Or maybe she's as good as Oprah Winfrey. In America, it's fashionable to be optimistic; in Europe, it's fashionable to be cynical. Cynicism never gets you anywhere. Dreaming does.

We should all accept that the food chain begins with the fox. Without an infusion of new foxes, no new wealth will be created; no small businesses will grow into large businesses; the tax receipts of the state will decline; new hospitals and schools will not be built; and teachers, nurses and other civil servants will be laid off because there is not enough money to pay their salaries. Hedgehogs need foxes more than foxes need hedgehogs! The cause of foxes, therefore, has to be embraced with passion – by the government and the private sector alike. Passion is what makes people allocate money and time to make things happen. When somebody says to me he hasn't got the time, I say: "No, you haven't got the passion. If you had the passion, you'd have the time." Passionless, lukewarm approval of foxes will get us nowhere. They are not a sideshow. They're the principal act.

An "ownership economy" is what foxes really desire. From childhood, we have the ambition to own something – model trains, dolls, a tricycle, Lego, whatever. Our possessions fulfil a deep, psychological need. A foxy society is one where ownership of land, homes, businesses, shares on the stock exchange, etc. is wholeheartedly pursued among all classes of the population. Owners don't want civil unrest, disruptions or crime to rob them of the things they have worked hard to own. As such, the development of a universal property-owning middle class is the ultimate stabilising force for society; and sound and enduring property rights are the foundation stone for an "ownership economy". It is an economy with a very different "architecture" to the one we have now. Clusters of small business units will dominate the economic landscape with a handful of smokestacks dotting the horizon. We shall have to get used to "creative destruction", a term coined by the great Austrian fox, Joseph Schumpeter, to describe how economies are transformed by technological innovation.

The sting in the tail for a democratically elected government is that when people become sufficiently miserable economically, anything can happen at the polls. Kohl was ousted by Schröder as Chancellor in the last German poll.

If Schröder doesn't bring down the unemployment rate, he'll go too. Roll back a few decades and, more dramatically, Hitler was elected by sufficiently miserable Germans in the mid-1930s.

So in any democracy, unless unemployment declines, look for a change in government as Vesuvius erupts at the polls and covers the incumbents with lava. If you accept my hypothesis that no new jobs (net) are going to be created in either the public or big business sector, then it has to be in an elected government's interest to make the medium-sized and small business sector their number one priority. Only then will the state make a real and lasting dent on unemployment. Mahatma Gandhi once said that mass production should mean production by the masses. Today that means millions of small enterprises like millions of flowers. Maybe some of them will grow to the size of Coca-Cola!

I have been advocating for some time in South Africa that the State President should award a monthly medal to an entrepreneur – such as the one I met in Khayelitsha. He should do it with maximum fanfare and media attention and proclaim unequivocally that the future of the country lies in the hands of the young foxes. Perhaps we should have the "Day of the Fox" once a year when small businesses around the land can display their wares and strut their stuff. Certainly, we should hold an annual national job creation competition where the winner is the company that has spawned the most entrepreneurs.

To be or not to be is not the question. To do or not to do is! Don't wait for the hedgehogs to do it for you. You'll be waiting till the end of the next millennium. Do it for yourself and do it in the next 24 hours. Whether you're a fox, a hedgehog or a hybrid of the two, life is no dress rehearsal. So the best advice to give is summed up in the refrain: "Live a lifetime in each minute, take the sweetness from within it." Maybe the tough times we are going through right now are the best prelude for a positive, foxy outlook to sweep the land. I can already smell the rain on the wind.

I hope I have entertained you with this book; but most of all I hope I have lit a fire in your soul to do something about it here in South Africa. Because, as a fox would say, it's only action that counts.